Essex*Works*.

For a better quality of life

Compiled by
by David Foster

Acknowledgements

Among the people who helped me research this book, I must mention Lee Skinner and Alex Russell, of Isle of Wight Council's Rights of Way office, and Tom Ransom, of Forest Enterprise. Robin Lang and Ian Ridett, of the National Trust, guided me through the difficult terrain at St Catherine's, and Colonel Aylmer kindly allowed me to photograph his home at Nunwell House. On a domestic note, Red Funnel, and WightLink ferries both went out of their way to ensure that my travel arrangements ran without a hitch.

Text:	David Foster
Photography:	David Foster
Editorial:	Ark Creative (UK) Ltd
Design:	Ark Creative (UK) Ltd

© Crimson Publishing, a division of Crimson Business Ltd

ISBN: 978-1-85458-522-6

While every care has been taken to ensure the accuracy of the route directions, the publishers cannot accept responsibility for errors or omissions, or for changes in details given. The countryside is not static: hedges and fences can be removed, field boundaries can alter, footpaths can be rerouted and changes in ownership can result in the closure or diversion of some concessionary paths. Also, paths that are easy and pleasant for walking in fine conditions may become slippery, muddy and difficult in wet weather, while stepping stones across rivers and streams may become impassable.

If you find an inaccuracy in either the text or maps, please write to Crimson Publishing at the address below.

First published 2004
Revised and reprinted 2007, 2008, 2010.

This edition first published in Great Britain 2010 by Crimson Publishing, a division of:
Crimson Business Ltd
Westminster House, Kew Road
Richmond, Surrey, TW9 2ND

www.totalwalking.co.uk

Printed in Singapore. 2/10

A catalogue record for this book is available from the British library.

Front cover: Freshwater Bay
Previous page: Brading High Street

Contents

Keymap

SCALE 1:217 500 or 1 INCH to 3½ MILES *1CM to 2.2KM*

| 0 | 2 | 4 | 6 | 8 | 10 | KILOMETRES | 15 |

| 0 | 2 | 4 | 6 | MILES | 8 | 10 |

KEYMAP HEIGHTS SHOWN IN METRES

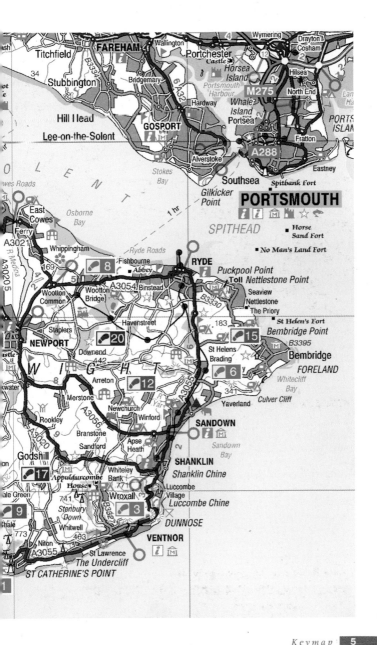

At-a-glance

1	2	3	4

To the lighthouse	*The old town at Newtown*	*Fur and feather at Wroxall*	*Fort Victoria*

• Spectacular views • lighthouse visits • rare wildlife • 16th century inn	• Lost town • birdwatching hide • river views • old town hall	• Donkey sanctuary • falconry centre • old railway path • ruined house	• Military history • coastal views • woodland trail • visitor attraction
Walk Distance 1¾ miles (2.8km) **Time** 1 hour **Refreshments** The Buddle Inn: real ales, home cooked food, garden	**Walk Distance** 2 miles (3.2km) **Time** 1 hour **Refreshments** None on the route, New Inn at Shalfleet is just a mile down the road	**Walk Distance** 2½ miles (4km) **Time** 1½ hours **Refreshments** The Worsley: Ushers beers, dining and family rooms, Aviary Café: hot and cold	**Walk Distance** 2½ miles (4km) **Time** 1½ hours **Refreshments** Verdi's café bar: snacks, hot meals, cream teas, ices, patio with superb coastal views
This route may become very muddy and slippery in wet weather, and many paths are not signposted. Camping and fires are prohibited, and visitors should keep dogs on leads	This is easy, level walking, some stiles. The route may be muddy in wet weather, coastal section may flood at the highest tides. *Please keep your dog on a lead throughout the walk*	Mostly easy walking, two stiles and a steep flight of steps. May be muddy. Please lead your dog through the donkey sanctuary; dogs are not allowed into the owl and falconry centre	This walk mainly follows roughly surfaced tracks. There are a handful of stiles, and the rural section may be muddy. *Please lead dogs near grazing animals, and scoop the poop in the country park*
p. 16	**p. 20**	**p. 24**	**p. 28**
Walk Completed ☑	Walk Completed ☐	Walk Completed ☐	Walk Completed ☐

5

Around Brighstone

6

Brading and Nunwell

7

West High Down

8

Wootton Bridge

• Pretty village • local museum • panoramic views • choice of pubs	• Historic town • country house • woods and park • toy museum	• Unrivalled views • cream teas • open-top bus • Needles Park	• Waterside pub • steam railway • rare wildlife • nice countryside

Walk Distance

2½ miles (4km)

Time

1½ hours

Refreshments

Three Bishops Free house. The Countryman, Brighstone tearooms

Walk Distance

2½ miles (4km)

Time

1½ hours

Refreshments

The Snooty Fox, Bugle Inn, Secret Garden tearoom, Brothers' fish and chip shop

Walk Distance

2½ miles (4km)

Time

1½ hours

Refreshments

Needles Park: hot meals; Warren Farm (seasonal): farmhouse cream teas

Walk Distance

2¾ miles (4.4km)

Time

1½ hours

Refreshments

The Sloop Inn (families welcome), The Cedars (play area)

This walk combines village and field edge paths with a bridleway route over high heathland. There are eight stiles, a fairly steep climb, and the route will be muddy in wet weather

Generally easy walking, though there are several stiles and the woods may be muddy. *Please lead dogs through Nunwell Farm, and through the grounds of Nunwell House*

The first half of this walk is one long, steady climb. *Take great care near unfenced cliffs, especially with children.* Please lead dogs near grazing animals

This easy-going route includes six stiles. *Please lead dogs through the fields at Mousehill Farm, and take particular care at the railway crossings*

p. 32   **p. 36**   **p. 40**   **p. 44**

Walk Completed ☐

Walk Completed ☐

Walk Completed ☐

Walk Completed ☐

9	10	11	12

Chale and Niton	*Mottistone and the coast*	*Freshwater and Tennyson Down*	*Newchurch*

• Blackgang Chine • glorious views • old lighthouse • Chale Farm ices	• Varied walking • standing stone • Gardens (NT) • Chilton Farm ices	• Superb views • famous landmark • popular beach • thatched church	• Historic church • young woodland • old railway path • nature trail

Walk Distance	**Walk Distance**	**Walk Distance**	**Walk Distance**
3½ miles (5.6km)	3¾ miles (6km)	3¾ miles (6km)	4 miles (6.4km)
Time	**Time**	**Time**	**Time**
2 hours	2 hours	2 hours	2 hours
Refreshments	**Refreshments**	**Refreshments**	**Refreshments**
Wight Mouse Inn, Chale. White Lion, Niton	Mottistone Manor tea garden; Isle of Wight Pearl coffee shop; ices at Chilton Farm	Freshwater Bay Tea Rooms; Albion Hotel; Tearoom at Dimbola Lodge	Pointer Inn: Gales ales, home-made food, family garden

Take care with children and dogs on sections that follow the A3055. There are a handful of stiles and a long climb up onto St Catherine's Hill; some sections may be muddy	This route climbs almost 350 ft from the coast to the Long Stone. There are seven stiles, and some sections may be muddy. *Please lead dogs through fields beyond Strawberry Lane*	Long and steady gradients, rather than steep. *Please take particular care near unfenced cliff edges especially with children.* Dogs on lead near grazing animals on the Down, and in Afton Marsh nature reserve	Generally easy walking, a few stiles, woodland sections may be muddy. Dogs on lead in churchyard, short sections of road, and Bembridge Trail and through newly planted woodland

p. 48	**p. 52**	**p.57**	**p. 62**
Walk Completed ☐	Walk Completed ☐	Walk Completed ☐	Walk Completed ☐

| 13 | 14 | 15 | 16 |

| *Carisbrooke and its castle* | *The western Yar* | *Around Bembridge* | *Beside the Medina* |

• Famous castle • downland views • causeway • varied scenery	• Yar Swing Bridge • historic castle • bird watching • old railway path	• Cliff walking • historic windmill • shady woodlands • sea views	• Riverside walk • all-weather path • nature reserve • bus ride

Walk Distance
4¼ miles (6.8km)
Time
2 hours
Refreshments
The Eight Bells: all day menu, garden, play area; The Waverley: bar food, garden

Please lead your dog through the farms and along White Lane, as well as in Carisbrooke village

Walk Distance
3¾ miles (6km)
Time
2 hours
Refreshments
The Red Lion, Freshwater. Yarmouth: Good selection of cafés and pubs

Active wheelchair users can enjoy the nicely surfaced outward route along the old Freshwater railway line. The return loop includes eight stiles, and follows signposted rural paths that may be muddy

Walk Distance
4¼ miles (6.8km)
Time
2 hours
Refreshments
Crab and Lobster, Pilot Boat Inn, Toll Gate café, Lifeboat View café

Generally easy walking, *but do take care where the path runs close to the clifftops*

Walk Distance
4½ miles (7.2km)
Time
2½ hours
Refreshments
Plenty in Newport and Cowes, no refreshment in between the two towns

The surface of this old railway cycle route is ideal for more adventurous wheelchair users. Fouling by dogs is an offence

p.66	p. 70	p. 74	p. 79
Walk Completed ☐	Walk Completed ☐	Walk Completed ☐	Walk Completed ☐

17

18

19

20

Godshill and Appuldurcombe

Newtown Harbour and Hamstead Point

Calbourne and Winkle Street

Steaming into Havenstreet

• Famous church	• Peaceful estuary	• Famous cottages	• Varied walking
• model village	• varied walking	• long views	• picnic areas
• cream teas	• coastal views	• forest trails	• heritage railway
• ruined house	• memorial	• mapping heritage	• woodlands

Walk Distance
5 miles (8km)
Time
2½ hours
Refreshments
Tea gardens Godshill; The Griffin, The Cask & Taverners, Appuldurcombe

Walk Distance
5 miles (8km)
Time
2½ hours
Refreshments
Horse & Groom, Ningwood: all-day menu, garden and play area

Walk Distance
5½ miles (8.8km)
Time
3 hours
Refreshments
The Sun: real ale, baguettes, jacket potatoes, hot meals, garden

Walk Distance
5½ miles (8.8km)
Time
3 hours
Refreshments
The White Hart: pub meals, garden, Havenstreet Station cafeteria

This strenuous walk climbs 600 ft to Stenbury Down. There are a handful of stiles, and the route may be muddy. *Please lead dogs through Godshill village, and near grazing animals*

Much of this remote route follows wide gravelled tracks, but *you'll also walk close to the water's edge and across low wooden causeways that may be submerged at high tide. The walk includes ten stiles*

With two strenuous climbs, poor signposting and a dozen stiles, this walk is not for the faint-hearted. Please lead dogs through farmland

This walk includes a dozen stiles and a mile of walking on country lanes, making it less suitable for groups or families with children. Please lead dogs along the roads, as well as through the farms

p. 84	p. 89	p. 94	p. 99

| Walk Completed ☑ | Walk Completed ☐ | Walk Completed ☐ | Walk Completed ☐ |

Introduction

Beyond Freshwater, the great white cliffs rise sheer from the English Channel. Here, the island narrows to a frail peninsula as the chalk ridge that stretches almost unbroken from its eastern extremity at Culver Cliff romps westwards over Tennyson Down to the Needles.

From his home at nearby Farringford, the Victorian poet laureate Alfred, Lord Tennyson, declared that the downland air was worth sixpence a pint. In today's money the price would be rather higher, for this is magical stuff. To be truthful, stepping out onto the coastal path in the golden light of a summer's evening is something like flying; your feet move easily over the close-cropped turf and, as you soar skywards on the westerly breeze, you can see almost 40 miles from Swanage to St Catherine's Point.

Inspiring landscapes

With its dramatic cliffs, wide-open river estuaries and rolling chalk downland, the Isle of Wight offers some of Britain's most diverse countryside. Ringed by nearly 30 miles of 'Heritage coasts', more than half the island is

Crossing Niton Down

officially designated as being of out-standing natural beauty. Away from the bustling seaside resorts, you'll find pretty lanes and thatched villages just waiting to welcome you – and, it's said, there's a pub for almost every square mile on the island.

More than 500 miles of carefully maintained footpaths make this the perfect destination for walkers. Here, walking is part of the culture. Eight waymarked leisure trails link the interior to the island's 67-mile coast path, and the Isle of Wight Council was the first authority in England to meet the Government's national rights-of-way target. No wonder that each May the Isle of Wight plays host to the UK's biggest walking festival.

Turbulent times

Long before these modern invasions, the island was captured by Vespasian and absorbed into the Roman Empire in the middle of the first century. The Romans built villas like the ones at Brading and Newport. They called their new territory Vectis – a name that you'll see every day on the side of Southern Vectis buses.

After the Romans left Britain some 400 years later, their place was taken by the West Saxons. The islanders endured foreign raids

St Agnes' Church, Freshwater Bay

throughout this turbulent period until, in 1066, the Norman Conquest heralded an era of political stability. King William's military commander founded the castle at Carisbrooke, as well as a number of island churches including the distinctive All Saints at Newchurch.

Years later, in 1256, the church itself took a hand in the island's development when the Bishop of Winchester established the port of Newtown. The town quickly grew prosperous and, for a time, it was the busiest port on the island; later, it fell victim to the old problem of foreign raids when the French destroyed it in 1377.

Further French incursions in the 16th century prompted Henry VIII to defend the island with a chain of forts such as the one at Yarmouth. History repeated itself in the Victorian era, and the government embarked on an extensive network of fortifications to protect Portsmouth's naval base from the old enemy. Island defences like the patriotically named Fort Victoria and Fort Albert were built to support a string of forts on the mainland and at Spithead.

A wildlife stronghold

If the Isle of Wight has borne its share of foreign invasions, it has so far remained secure against a more insidious assault. The American grey squirrel was introduced to Britain in the 1870s and, by the mid-20th century, it had driven native red squirrels from most parts of the mainland. Today, the Isle of Wight is one of the few places in southern England where you can see this engaging creature in its natural habitat.

The island is also the last British stronghold of the attractive Glanville fritillary butterfly, and a small colony of reddish-buff moths near Newtown Harbour is the only native population of its kind anywhere in Britain. Low-lying estuaries and mudflats at

Newtown, Yarmouth and along the Medina are great places for wildlife, and birdwatchers may see waterfowl such as little egret, curlew, redshank or black-tailed godwit.

In fact, the island is something of a naturalist's paradise. The southern coastline contains more than 20 miles of naturally developing soft cliffs, an internationally rare habitat protected by European legislation. Often called the Dinosaur Coast, this crumbling coastline is rich in fossils, as well as rare insects and colourful plants like field cow-wheat, hoary stock and ivy broomrape.

Yarmouth tide mill (1793)

Winners and Losers

You'll witness the dramatic effects of this natural erosion on several of the walks, and it's not surprising that coastal protection is a thorny issue on an island that has been changing its shape since prehistoric times. Realigning the coastal path may be relatively straightforward, but regular landslips also threaten sections of the Military Road between Niton and Freshwater.

Attractions like Isle of Wight Pearl stand close to the retreating cliffs and the gardens at Blackgang Chine are now much smaller than when they were first laid out in the 1840s. In contrast, the inland walks will bring you to historic buildings like Appuldurcombe House, Bembridge windmill and Newtown town hall that have been saved from collapse through the ravages of time. The Isle of Wight steam railway is another success story, with three times as much track as it had in 1990.

With so much to see, you may be wondering where to start. If you're already on the island, you'll probably want to begin with a nearby walk – but don't forget that with up to 350 ferry crossings a day, the Isle of Wight makes a great day out from the mainland. Three of the walks in this book start close to the main ferry terminals, and there are also good public transport links to the rest of the island.

So lace up your boots and dig out the maps – you don't want to miss the boat.

This book includes a list of waypoints alongside the description of the walk, so that you can enjoy the full benefits of gps should you wish to.

For more information on using your gps, read the *Pathfinder® Guide GPS for Walkers*, by gps teacher and navigation trainer, Clive Thomas (ISBN 978-0-7117-4445-5).

For essential information on map reading and basic navigation, read the *Pathfinder® Guide Map Reading Skills* by outdoor writer, Terry Marsh (ISBN 978-0-7117-4978-8). Both titles are available in bookshops or can be ordered online at www.totalwalking.co.uk

To the lighthouse

- Spectacular views
- lighthouse visits
- rare wildlife
- 16th century inn

walk 1

The route begins by dropping down through the contorted National Trust landscape to reach the lighthouse road. There is a pleasant walk through the fields above St Catherine's Point, before joining Castlehaven Lane for the climb to the Buddle Inn. A gentle section along leafy Old Blackgang Road completes the circuit.

St Catherine's Lighthouse

walk 1

START Windy Gap car park, Old Blackgang Road

DISTANCE 1¾ miles (2.8km)

TIME 1 hour

PARKING At the start

ROUTE FEATURES This route may become very muddy and slippery in wet weather, and many paths are not signposted. Camping and fires are prohibited, and visitors should keep dogs on leads

GPS WAYPOINTS
 SZ 494 758
Ⓐ SZ 500 756
Ⓑ SZ 505 758

PUBLIC TRANSPORT Limited bus service from Newport and Ventnor to the Buddle Inn (0871 200 2233)

REFRESHMENTS The Buddle Inn: real ales, home cooked food, garden

PUBLIC TOILETS None

ORDNANCE SURVEY MAPS Explorer OL29 (Isle of Wight)

 Leave the car park by the kissing-gate that was on your left as you drove into the car park, and follow the undulating path for 90 yds. Here, a sea view opens up on your right and there is a shallow valley running away to the left. Turn along the valley, and walk between the rocky outcrops and low trees for 160 yds until you come to a fork in the path. Keep right here, climbing steeply for a few paces through a gap in the trees, for your first view of the gleaming white lighthouse below. Now bear left and follow the path as it winds along the hillside with good coastal views to your right. Just beyond a small concrete survey pillar the path enters an area of scrubby bushes and drops steadily down to a wire fence. Bear right, and continue for the last 60 yds to a gate and stile leading you out onto the lighthouse road **Ⓐ**.

Nip over the stile and turn right down the hill, until you reach a large pair of stone gate

> **Chale Bay** and **St Catherine's** was notorious for wrecks, with a record 14 losses on a single night in 1757. Although the 14th-century lighthouse on St Catherine's Hill *(see Walk 9)* was operational for some 200 years, it was often obscured by fog at the very times when it was most needed. The present lighthouse was built in 1840, following the wreck of the *Clarendon* in 1837. It is open to the public, and guided tours last 35 minutes.

Buddle Inn

pillars on the left-hand side. The prominent local Kirkpatrick family built the pillars in the first half of the 19th century as a grand entrance for a summer residence. However, because of the site's exposed location, the house itself was never built. Instead, the family built Windcliff, farther up the hill, in 1840.

Turn between the pillars and through a kissing-gate onto footpath NT40 towards Castlehaven Lane. Follow the hedge on your left through a gap beside an old kissing-gate, and continue through the next gate on your left onto an enclosed path for the short remaining distance to Castlehaven Lane.

? *Who was the most famous resident of Knowles Farm House?*

Fork left up the hill, pass the Old Radio Station and Wireless Cottage, and follow the lane as it bears left and climbs to the junction with St Catherine's Road **B**.

Residents in Castlehaven are not immune to the general threat of landslips along the island's southern coast. In recent years, several

properties have suffered from subsidence triggered by groundwater lubricating the underlying clay, and the Military Road was re-routed following a major landslip in 2002. The large number of manholes in Castlehaven Lane and St Catherine's Road were installed in 2004 as part of a £5.9 million land drainage and coast protection scheme. The project includes a 20-acre nature reserve to help mitigate the effect on the area's outstanding local wildlife.

Niton Undercliff – the area between the towering inland cliffs and the sea – is one of the most unstable sections of the Island's steadily eroding south-west coastline. Powerful landslips have created the dramatic, contorted scenery, and the constantly disturbed soil is home to many unusual plants and insects. Wild liquorice and tufted centaury both grow on the National Trust's estate, which also supports a colony of the rare Glanville fritillary butterfly.

Turn left along St Catherine's Road to the Buddle Inn on your right-hand side. Just here, turn right up the signposted footpath beside the pub garden. Turn left at the top, and follow the road round to its junction with Old Blackgang Road. Turn right, and follow the leafy old road back to the start of your walk.

The old town at Newtown

- Lost town
- birdwatching hide
- river views
- old town hall

walk 2

This varied route weaves its way around the grassy tracks and paths that once formed Newtown's busy thoroughfares. There's a short section on a quiet country road, but for most of the way you'll follow attractive green lanes and waterside paths through the glorious landscape of Newtown Harbour National Nature Reserve.

Newtown, Causeway Lake

walk 2

START Old town hall, Newtown

DISTANCE 2 miles (3.2km)

TIME 1 hour

PARKING National Trust car park opposite the town hall

ROUTE FEATURES This is easy, level walking, although there are half a dozen stiles. The route may become muddy in wet weather, and the coastal section may flood at the highest tides. *Please keep your dog on a lead throughout the walk*

GPS WAYPOINTS
📍 SZ 423 906
Ⓐ SZ 429 904
Ⓑ SZ 421 907
Ⓒ SZ 423 904

PUBLIC TRANSPORT Buses from Newport and Yarmouth to Shalfleet (0871 200 2233)

REFRESHMENTS None on the route, but the popular New Inn at Shalfleet is just a mile down the road

PUBLIC TOILETS At the start

ORDNANCE SURVEY MAPS Explorer OL29 (Isle of Wight)

Turn left out of the car park and, after 60 yds, turn right through the signposted kissing-gate beside the former Francheville Arms. This lovely green lane runs between hedges of dog rose, bramble and willow and was once part of Newtown's High Street. Cross the waymarked stile, then zigzag right and left through a gap in the hedge and continue over a second waymarked stile. Walk through a gap in the hedge straight ahead of you, then simply follow the waymarked route through a small finger of woodland and out through a kissing-gate onto a country lane Ⓐ.

Turn left, follow the road around the left-hand bend, and continue for 600 yds to the next left-hand bend. Jump the stile in front of you here, and continue between the hedges that fringe the former Gold Street, now a pleasant green lane, until you reach the stile at the far end Ⓑ.

Cross over the stile and, after just a few paces, turn right along the signposted footpath up the gated lane past Marsh Farm House. Continue past a second gate onto a hedged footpath that leads out to the wooden bird

? *What was the rent for a house and garden when Newtown was first established in 1256?*

hide at the edge of the marsh, where the warden keeps a chalk board list of species seen on the reserve. Take your binoculars, and you may see little egret, pintail and ringed plover – not to mention butterflies like the painted lady and speckled wood.

In medieval times, **Newtown** was the Island's principal port. With its prosperous merchants and tradesmen, its salt pans and its oyster fishery, Newtown was assessed at twice the value of Newport. But things changed: the French sacked the town in 1377, the harbour silted up, and the ships came no more. Today, just a handful of houses, a redundant town hall and a network of green lanes are all that are left of Newtown's flourishing past.

Turn left at the hide, go through a kissing-gate, and continue until you reach a gap in the hedge near the end of a long wooden causeway. Turn left again, go through a kissing-gate, and follow the path up the side of the hay meadows with a hedge on your left-hand side. The path turns left through a small wooden gate and returns to the road at the Old Coastguard Station, now a private house.

The old town hall.

Follow the road around the right-hand bend, briefly retracing your steps at point **B** until the road swings away to the left at the Church of the Holy Spirit. Just here, take the signposted footpath straight ahead, go through a kissing-gate, and bear left across the hay meadows. There's a glorious vista across the Causeway Lake as the path drops down and bears left along the waterfront to a kissing-gate. Continue for 75 yds to meet the road at a gap in the hedge near a bench seat on your left **C**.

Newtown's old town hall was an early beneficiary of the mysterious **Ferguson's Gang**. This bizarre band of anonymous National Trust supporters was formed in 1927, and their first project was to raise funds for Shalford Mill in Surrey. The **masked gang members**, who were known by pseudonyms like 'Bill Stickers', 'The Bishop' and 'Red Biddy', bought the town hall for £5 and gave it to the National Trust in 1933. Later, the gang raised £1,000 to restore the building.

Turn left up Town Lane to return to the car park opposite the town hall.

Fur and feather at Wroxall

- Donkey sanctuary
- falconry centre
- old railway path
- ruined house

walk 3

The walk heads north along the old Ventnor to Shanklin railway line before turning across country through the donkey sanctuary to Freemantle Gate. From here it's easy going to the owl and falconry centre at Appuldurcombe House (see Walk 17), before dropping back down to Wroxall for the short homeward stretch on the old railway.

Wroxall, Isle of Wight Donkey Sanctuary

walk 3

START St Martins Road, Wroxall

DISTANCE 2½ miles (4km)

TIME 1½ hours

PARKING At the start

ROUTE FEATURES Mostly easy walking with just two stiles and a steep flight of steps. Some sections may be muddy. Please lead your dog through the donkey sanctuary; *dogs are not allowed into the owl and falconry centre*

GPS WAYPOINTS
- SZ 551 798
- Ⓐ SZ 551 810
- Ⓑ SZ 540 807
- Ⓒ SZ 542 801

PUBLIC TRANSPORT Regular bus service from all the main Island towns (0871 200 2233)

REFRESHMENTS The Worsley: Ushers beers, dining and family rooms, Aviary Café: hot and cold drinks/lunches

PUBLIC TOILETS Wroxall village centre and Appuldurcombe House

ORDNANCE SURVEY MAPS Explorer OL29 (Isle of Wight)

Turn left out of the car park and walk down to the B3327 opposite The Worsley. Turn right past St John's Church, then right again up Castle Road. Just before the old railway bridge, turn left onto the footpath towards Shanklin and drop down past the industrial buildings onto the old railway line. Follow the track as it pulls away from the village, passes Yard Farm on your right, and runs through a shallow cutting.

Now, look out for a gate and stile on your left Ⓐ; nip across, and walk down through the small field to a second stile and footpath signpost. Go over the stile and continue down a surfaced lane to the main road, taking care as you zigzag right and left across the road to join the bridleway towards Redhill Lane. The route continues through the Isle of Wight Donkey Sanctuary, leaving the site at a wooden five-bar gate.

Cross the wooden footbridge, then bear right along the signposted bridleway GL36. The track winds through a small wooden gate, and emerges from a patch of trees to run along the right-hand side of an open field. There are good views of Appuldurcombe Down on the

? *What is the full dedication of St John's Church, Wroxall?*

left, before another small gate marks the start of a path that leads you out between hedges to Redhill Lane. Zigzag left and right across the lane and join bridleway GL49 towards Stenbury Down for the waymarked climb to a five-bar gate at Freemantle Copse **B**.

Turn left just beyond the gate, and follow the bridleway towards Wroxall through the imposing Freemantle Gate at the edge of the

Appuldurcombe, Freemantle Gate

Appuldurcombe estate. One hundred yards farther on, bear right along the main gravelled track towards Appuldurcombe House and continue to the car park opposite the entrance to the owl and falconry centre **C**.

Turn left at the car park and follow the drive as it leads away from Appuldurcombe House. Bear right onto Appuldurcombe Road, and continue to the main B3327. Go carefully as you zigzag right and left across the main road, then climb the steep wooden steps to rejoin the old railway. Turn right, and retrace your outward steps back to Wroxall village and the car park where your walk began.

> ✱ Falconry is one of the world's oldest sports, and was a favourite with King Henry VIII when he visited **Appuldurcombe House** *(see Walk 17)* in 1539. **The Isle of Wight Owl and Falconry Centre** at Appuldurcombe features flying displays with raptors from around the world, as well as aviaries containing owls, falcons, hawks, vultures and kites. There's an indoor flight barn for wet days, as well as a souvenir shop and Aviary Café.

Fort Victoria

■ **Military history** ■ **woodland nature trail**
■ **coastal views** ■ **visitor attractions**

Starting from Fort Victoria Country Park, the walk follows the coastal path to the outskirts of Yarmouth. After doubling back across grazing fields you'll rejoin the coastal path for the return to Fort Victoria, where there's a good range of facilities and family attractions.

walk 4

Fort Victoria café bar

walk 4

START Fort Victoria Country Park

DISTANCE 2½ miles (4km)

TIME 1½ hours

PARKING At the start

ROUTE FEATURES This walk mainly follows roughly surfaced tracks. There are a handful of stiles, and the rural section may be muddy. *Please lead dogs near grazing animals*

GPS WAYPOINTS
- SZ 338 897
- Ⓐ SZ 347 896
- Ⓑ SZ 344 893
- Ⓒ SZ 333 887

PUBLIC TRANSPORT Bus services from Yarmouth and Freshwater (0871 200 2233)

REFRESHMENTS Verdi's café bar: snacks, light lunches, hot meals, cream teas, ices, patio with superb coastal views

PUBLIC TOILETS At the start

ORDNANCE SURVEY MAPS Explorer OL29 (Isle of Wight)

Face the fort and walk around the left-hand end by the toilets. Turn left after 50 yds, signposted towards the coastal path and nature trail, and climb up through the woods to the coastal path. Turn left along the roughly surfaced woodland track, passing the backs of some houses on your left. Bear right when you meet the access road to the fort, follow it for 100 yds, then continue along the coastal path as it bears off to the left towards Yarmouth.

The path will lead you through a small patch of woodland before dropping down a couple of steps and turning right along the sea wall. Here you'll enjoy good views of St James' Church tower standing sentinel above the little town of Yarmouth and its attractive harbour. Bear right as you reach the information panel at Norton Spit Site of Special Scientific Interest, and continue to the main road at Halletts Shute Ⓐ.

> **?** *Where might you see marram grass, sea lavender and sea holly?*

Cross over and turn left along the pavement for 80 yds. Now turn right down Gasworks Lane and follow the Freshwater Way until you reach a stile on your right, just beyond Norlands Cottage. Nip across, and follow footpath F2 as it branches off towards Halletts Shute, following the hedge on your right-hand side. A second stile leads you along a narrow enclosed path to meet the main road, where you turn left along the pavement.

Take the first turning on your right into Westhill Lane **B**, signposted towards the Fort Victoria Country Park. Pass Braxton Meadow on your left, cross the little white-railed bridge, then turn left into Linstone Drive

> ⁕ **Fort Victoria** was part of a chain of defences commissioned by Queen Victoria to protect the Solent against the French. The buildings were completed in 1855, but more powerful naval guns quickly rendered them obsolete and the fort was later converted into a submarine mining depot. You can see a short section of tramway from this period in the car park. The fort was originally triangular, but the large barrack blocks on the third side were demolished in 1969.

along footpath F3 towards Colwell. As the road bears around to the right, go off to the left along a grassy lane and through a wooden kissing-gate into a long narrow field.

The Solent and Hurst Castle from the coastal path

Elder, dog-rose, blackthorn and gorse are your companions as you follow the right-hand hedge through an opening beside a stile into the next field. Here the path swings across to follow the left-hand hedge until an indistinct trackway crosses your path through a field gate on the left. Go over the stile in front of you, and continue along the right-hand side of the next field until you reach another stile **C**.

BOAT

Cross the stile and turn right onto the signposted coastal path along Monks Lane until you reach the entrance to a distinctive row of bungalows at Cliff End. Just here, dodge away to your right and follow the coastal path as it winds between the fences around the edge of the housing estate. Soon the path turns right, shakes off the houses, and continues into the wooded country park. There are bench seats here and lovely views across the Solent towards Hurst Castle.

> A woodland nature trail now follows part of the old military road that once linked Fort Victoria to Fort Albert – you can pick up a trail guide from the Ranger Base near the start of this walk. More formal attractions at the Fort include the **Island Planetarium** and a marine aquarium, as well as the **Sunken History** exhibition and a model railway.

Drop down a flight of steps, and continue for 600 yds through the woods to a signposted fork in the track. Turn left here, towards the refreshments and toilets, for the short way back to the fort. ◼

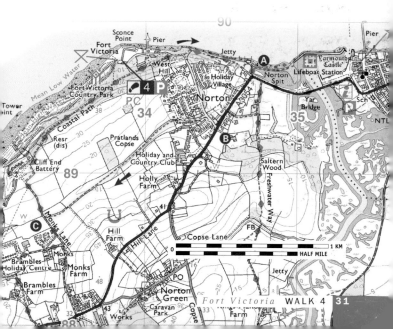

Around Brighstone

■ **Pretty village**　　　■ **panoramic views**
■ **local museum**　　　■ **choice of pubs**

The walk heads south past Brighstone Mill before picking its way across farmland to the church and on towards The Countryman. Now you'll climb steeply onto heathland in the hills behind the village, where you can look down on your route through the landscape below. An attractive bridleway leads you back to the village and its museum.

walk 5

Brighstone museum, cottage tableau

walk 5

START Warnes Lane car park.

DISTANCE 2½ miles (4km)

TIME 1½ hour

PARKING At the start

ROUTE FEATURES This walk combines village and field edge paths with a bridleway route over high heathland. There are eight stiles, a fairly steep climb, and the route will be muddy in wet weather

GPS WAYPOINTS

🖉 SZ 427 827
Ⓐ SZ 427 821
Ⓑ SZ 436 826
Ⓒ SZ 433 832

PUBLIC TRANSPORT Bus services from Newport, Yarmouth and Freshwater (0871 200 2233)

REFRESHMENTS Three Bishops: Free house (all day family menu) The Countryman: Free house (home cooked food) Brighstone tearooms

PUBLIC TOILETS At the start

PLAY AREA None

ORDNANCE SURVEY MAPS Explorer OL29 (Isle of Wight)

🖉 Leave the car park on footpath BS25 towards Galley Lane and follow it out to the Methodist Church. Bear left into Wilberforce Road, then zigzag right and left onto a signposted footpath. Cross the plank bridge, go through the kissing-gate, and follow the path as it winds beside an attractive brook and through a second kissing-gate to Brighstone Mill. Turn left onto Wicken Hill Lane and continue for 200 yds to a signposted footpath on your left Ⓐ.

> ✳ Brighstone has links with **William Wilberforce**, the 19th-century philanthropist who was influential in ending the slave trade. His son, Samuel Wilberforce, was the Rector of Brighstone during the 1830s, and William Wilberforce was a familiar sight in the village in the last years of his life. The family name is perpetuated in Wilberforce Road and the Wilberforce Hall.

Nip over the stile and follow the left-hand field edge. A further two stiles carry you behind the buildings at Waytes Court, where the path bears left. Continue over another stile and a wooden footbridge, and continue until you reach the main road near the church. Turn right along the main road for the short distance past Bakehouse Cottage to the junction with Broad Lane.

The track off the Downs

Cross the stile on the far side of the road and turn immediately right, following footpath BS21 along the field edge towards Yafford. Keep the hedge on your right as the path bears to the left, then gently back to the right. Bear right over two stiles when you reach the corner of the field and keep walking in the same direction, now with a hedge on your left, until you reach a stile 275 yds farther on. Turn left over the stile and continue along the right-hand field edge until, just beyond a pair of wooden gates, you meet the main road beside Brighstone Parish Cemetery **B**.

Cross the road and turn left along the grass verge; then, immediately past The Countryman, turn right up the signposted 'bridleway BS31 towards Brighstone Forest'. The green track climbs between wire fences, then bears left through an attractive tunnel of wind-sculpted trees and climbs more steeply to a lonely wooden signpost **C**.

Turn left here, along bridleway BS34 towards Brighstone. Now the views make up for the climb, with a wide sweep from St Catherine's Hill almost to the Needles. Brighstone itself is laid out like a map at your feet and it's easy to pick out the way that you've walked. The sandy track drops through a sunken way fringed with bracken and gorse,

> There's an attractive row of National Trust thatched cottages in **North Street**, containing the Post Office and National Trust shop, as well as a locally run **village museum**. Here you can see typical domestic items from the 19th century in a cottage tableau that includes an early sewing machine, bread oven and 'pegged' rug. Other displays focus on farming, land management and the village school.

then swings
to the left and continues
between tall hedgerow trees back
into the village. Cross straight
over into North Street, pass the

> **?** *When was Brighstone's Wilberforce Church hall built?*

museum and National Trust shop, then zigzag across the main road into
Warnes Lane for the last few yards back to your car. ∎

National Trust cottages, North Street

Brading and Nunwell

- Historic town
- country house
- woods and parkland
- toy museum

walk 6

Starting from the heart of the little town, the walk uses footpaths and bridleways to complete a circuit of the Nunwell estate. There's a mix of scenery, from field edge paths and woodland tracks to a parkland finale with good views of Nunwell House.

Brading High Street

walk 6

START High Street, just north of the church

DISTANCE 2½ miles (4km)

TIME 1½ hours

PARKING Pay and Display car park at the start

ROUTE FEATURES Generally easy walking, though there are several stiles and the woods may be muddy. *Please lead dogs through Nunwell Farm, and through the grounds of Nunwell House*

GPS WAYPOINTS

🖉 SZ 606 874
Ⓐ SZ 600 870
Ⓑ SZ 592 872
Ⓒ SZ 591 878
Ⓓ SZ 601 875

PUBLIC TRANSPORT Island Line trains (0845 748 4950) also buses from Newport, Ryde, Sandown, Shanklin and Ventnor (0871 200 2233)

REFRESHMENTS The Snooty Fox and the Bugle Inn, the Secret Garden tearooms, and Brothers' traditional fish and chip shop

PUBLIC TOILETS At the start

ORDNANCE SURVEY MAPS Explorer OL29 (Isle of Wight)

🖉 Turn left out of the car park, cross the High Street and continue for 75 yds beyond the church. Turn right into Cross Street, then right again at the end, up a surfaced path with houses on your right. A few paces before the path meets West Lane, turn left onto footpath B27 towards Brading Down, following the edge of an open field with hedgerow trees on your right.

> **?** *How many exhibits are there in the Lilliput antique doll and toy museum?*

Cross the stile at the top corner of the field Ⓐ and turn immediately right. After a few more paces the path merges with a wider bridleway that sweeps in from your left; join it, and continue through the woods until you reach a three-way wooden signpost. The Nunwell oaks were used for shipbuilding in Tudor and Napoleonic times, as well as for construction timbers in local manor houses. These woods were badly damaged in the great storm of October 1987, but have been extensively replanted.

Ⓑ Turn right here onto bridleway B59 towards Nunwell and Hardingshute. Follow the track as it swings left past a substantial lodge cottage, where the trail becomes a

surfaced lane. Pass
Nunwell Farm and
continue for 150 yds
to a stile on your
right **C**.

There's plenty to see in and around Brading. Your route passes St Mary's Church and the **Lilliput Toy Museum**, as well as the Isle of Wight Wax Works with its **Chamber of Horrors** and candle carving demonstrations. And, within half a mile, you could take in the elegant Georgian Morton Manor, Adgestone vineyard, and the magnificent remains of Brading Roman villa.

Nip over the stile and
follow the signposted
footpath B23 across open pasture towards Brading. Cross a plank bridge
and stile beneath a massive old oak tree, and bear gently left past a
waymarked oak tree on the crest of a low hill until you reach a footpath
signpost 200 yds farther on. There are good views of Nunwell House on

Nunwell House, east front

this section, *but do please respect the owner's privacy and keep to the public footpath.* Continue over a stile, still following the signposted path towards Brading as it tracks a rough line of oak trees heading just to the left of the lodge cottage on West Lane.

The plank bridge and stile beside the cottage will lead you out onto West Lane **D**. *There's no pavement here, so take care as you turn right* and continue for 80 yds beyond the entrance to Nunwell House. Turn right into Doctors Lane and retrace your outward steps back to the start.

> **Nunwell House** was the ancestral home of the influential Oglander family from 1522, and King Charles I spent his last night of freedom here during the Civil War. More recently, the **East Wight Home Guard** was based at Nunwell in the Second World War, and a small museum now commemorates this period. The house was bought by Colonel and Mrs Aylmer in 1982, and is open three days a week in the summer months.

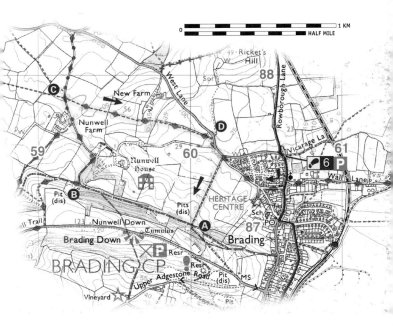

West High Down

- Unrivalled views
- cream teas
- open-top bus
- Needles Park

walk 7

Starting from Alum Bay, the walk makes a complete circuit of West High Down, the dramatic chalk headland that culminates at the Needles. The walk itself takes just 1½ hours, but you could easily spend half a day exploring the Needles headland and its attractions, or link the route with Walk 11 for a full day out.

Alum Bay from the coastal path

walk 7

START The Needles Park, Alum Bay

DISTANCE 2½ miles (4km)

TIME 1½ hours

PARKING Large car park at the start (charges vary)

ROUTE FEATURES The first half of this walk is one long, steady climb. *Take great care near unfenced cliffs, especially with children.* Please lead dogs near grazing animals

GPS WAYPOINTS
- SZ 307 853
- **Ⓐ** SZ 302 849
- **Ⓑ** SZ 306 849
- **Ⓒ** SZ 318 853

PUBLIC TRANSPORT Buses from all the main Island towns, also frequent open-top service from Yarmouth (0871 200 2233)

REFRESHMENTS Needles Park: snacks, hot meals, licensed bar; Warren Farm (seasonal): sandwich lunches, farmhouse cream teas

PUBLIC TOILETS At the start

ORDNANCE SURVEY MAPS Explorer OL29 (Isle of Wight)

From the miniature lighthouse at the car park entrance, set off up the coastal path along the sign-posted road towards the Needles Old Battery and tearoom. Follow the road around to the right and continue for almost ½ mile as it climbs towards the Old Battery. All the way along this section you'll enjoy spectacular views of Alum Bay, the Solent and Hurst Castle.

Bear left at the coastal footpath sign **Ⓐ**, following the narrow chalk path that climbs steeply away from the road towards the old Coastguard Cottages. Just below the cottages, the coastal path doubles back at a stile and climbs to the crest of West High Down, opening up a stunning 360-degree panorama all the way from Dorset to St Catherine's Point. Bear left along the top of the ridge, heading just a few degrees to the left of Tennyson's Monument, a mile or so in front of you.

> **?** *What replaced the original Nodes Beacon?*

Pass the small War Department marker stone on the summit **Ⓑ**, and follow the downland track as it drops down the ridge, still aiming slightly to the north of Tennyson's Monument. Clumps of gorse now dot the

THIS STONE
MARKS THE SITE OF THE
NEEDLES
WIRELESS TELEGRAPH STATION
WHERE
GUGLIELMO MARCONI
AND HIS BRITISH COLLABORATORS
CARRIED OUT FROM
6TH DECEMBER 1897
TO 26TH MAY 1900
A SERIES OF EXPERIMENTS
WHICH CONSTITUTED SOME OF
THE MORE IMPORTANT PHASES
OF THEIR EARLIER PIONEER
WORK IN THE DEVELOPMENT OF
WIRELESS COMMUNICATION
OF ALL KINDS.

This small memorial at the Needles Park marks the spot where **Guglielmo Marconi** and his British associates established an experimental wireless telegraphy station in 1897. The station was based at the Needles Hotel, and Lord Kelvin made history here when he sent the first commercial radio telegram in June 1898. Eighteen months later, Marconi broadcast information to the United States liner *St Paul* for the first newspaper ever produced and printed at sea.

landscape as the track heads decisively towards the edge of the woods at the back of Tennyson Down. At the foot of the slope you'll come to a stile, right beside a wooden replica of the old Nodes beacon.

Until it was taken down in 1897, the Nodes Beacon was a well-known local landmark that still features on the seal of Totland Parish Council. The Rotary Club of West Wight erected this half-size replica beside a

Nodes Beacon

fragment of the original beacon to mark the Queen's Silver Jubilee in 1977.

Just a few paces short of the stile **C**, swing hard left onto footpath T25, signposted towards Alum Bay.

The path drops gently down through the gorse bushes, passes a worked-out chalk pit and dives through a small thicket. Now there's a wire fence in the hedge on your right-hand side and, in just under ½ mile, you'll

reach the gate to Warren Farm, nestling peacefully in the sequestered valley on your right. It's well worth dropping in here for a light lunch or traditional cream tea during the season when the farm is open. Beyond Warren Farm, simply follow the fence until you reach a stile straight in front of you. Nip across, drop down a dozen steps, and turn right onto the road to return to your car. ■

Wootton Bridge

■ **Waterside pub** ■ **rare wildlife**

■ **steam railway** ■ **unspoiled countryside**

walk 8

This delightful walk is a favourite with railway enthusiasts, and offers glimpses of Wootton Station as it pushes out into lovely, unspoiled countryside. The route crosses the line twice before turning north through light woodland to reach the Old Mill Pond and Wootton Creek.

No 198 Royal Engineer *heads a train near Ashey*

walk 8

START Car park in Brannon Way (turning opposite Tesco Express)

DISTANCE 2¾ miles (4.4km)

TIME 1½ hours

PARKING Free car park at the start

ROUTE FEATURES This easy-going route includes six stiles. *Please lead dogs through the fields at Mousehill Farm, and take particular care at the railway crossings*

GPS WAYPOINTS

  SZ 543 919
Ⓐ SZ 538 910
Ⓑ SZ 536 905
Ⓒ SZ 543 904
Ⓓ SZ 546 919

PUBLIC TRANSPORT Buses from Cowes, Newport and Ryde (0871 200 2233). Isle of Wight steam railway trains (01983 882204)

REFRESHMENTS The Sloop Inn (families welcome), The Cedars (play area)

PUBLIC TOILETS At the start

ORDNANCE SURVEY MAPS Explorer OL29 (Isle of Wight)

Turn right out of the car park, then left onto the main road opposite Tesco Express, and set off up the hill. Turn left into Station Road when you reach The Cedars, then take the second turning on the left into Packsfield Lane. A few houses line the route at first, but soon you'll find yourself treading an attractive lane between hedges of beech, holly, oak and bramble, with glimpses of Wootton Station away to the right. The well-surfaced path narrows and climbs gently past Packsfield Farmhouse to the gated railway crossing.

Keep a good look out for trains as you cross the line **Ⓐ** and fork left onto the narrow bridleway N7, signposted towards Littletown Lane. Zigzag right, then left, at Woodford Cottage and continue to the T-junction with bridleway N3. Turn left towards Briddlesford Road, following the lane as it swings to the right in front of the white-painted 'Shiloh'.

> **The Ryde and Newport Railway** opened the line from Smallbrook Junction to Newport in 1875. The original platform at Wootton was west of Station Road, with an unusual booking office and waiting room built into an arch of the road bridge. Landslips led to the closure of this station in 1953 and, following preservation work, the Isle of Wight Steam Railway opened a new terminus on the present site in 1986.

Wootton Station, signal box

Pass Little Mousehill Farm
Cottage and turn left over the stile
B along footpath N2, signposted
towards Woodhouse Farm.
Continue over three more stiles
into a small wood, tracking the
woodland edge until the path
breaks clear at a waymarked stile.
Bear gently right here along the
side of the next field, go over the
stile in the far corner, and turn left
along bridleway N1 towards
Wootton Bridge **C**.

Several of the woodlands
south of Wootton Bridge
are included within the
**Briddlesford Copses Site of
Special Scientific Interest**. This
official designation puts them
among England's finest wildlife
locations, legally protected by
Natural England. Beyond the
second railway crossing the route
passes through Hurst Copse,
notable for hornbeam, alder and
wild service trees, as well as
dormice, red squirrels, and eight
species of bats.

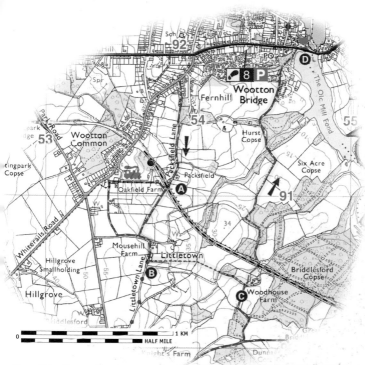

Keep Woodhouse Farm to your
right as you drop down
and bear right to the railway
crossing. *Watch out for trains as
you cross the line once again*, then

**? What is the penalty
for trespassing on
the railway?**

bear left and follow the lane as it winds its way north through a
patchwork of woods and fields. Take the chance to explore the wildlife
as you pass Hurst Copse on your right, or simply continue until you
reach the pretty Fernhill Farm on your left-hand side. Here the lane
becomes a surfaced drive as it runs close to the Old Mill Pond for the
remaining short distance to the Sloop Inn **D**.

Turn left opposite the Sloop and follow the main road up through
Wootton Bridge as far as Tesco Express on your right. Turn left into
Brannon Way to return to your car. ■

Chale and Niton

- Blackgang Chine
- glorious views
- medieval lighthouse
- Chale Farm ice creams

walk 9

A gentle stroll through Chale village leads you to a short section of the coastal path and the attractions at Blackgang Chine. Soon the walk cuts inland along a charming bridleway to Niton before climbing steadily over the flank of St Catherine's Down and dropping back into Chale.

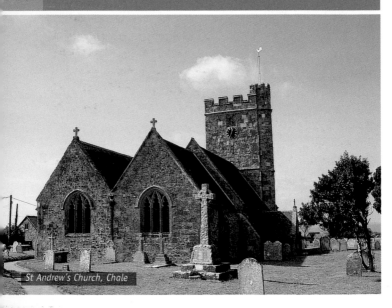

St Andrew's Church, Chale

walk 9

START Chale village car park

DISTANCE 3½ miles (5.6km)

TIME 2 hours

PARKING At the start

ROUTE FEATURES *Take care with children and dogs on sections that follow the A3055. There are a handful of stiles and a long climb up onto St Catherine's Hill; some sections may be muddy*

GPS WAYPOINTS
- SZ 484 778
- **A** SZ 488 769
- **B** SZ 492 764
- **C** SZ 502 766
- **D** SZ 500 774
- **E** SZ 492 777

PUBLIC TRANSPORT Bus services from Newport and Ventnor (0871 200 2233)

REFRESHMENTS Wight Mouse Inn, Chale. White Lion, Niton

PUBLIC TOILETS Niton village

ORDNANCE SURVEY MAPS Explorer OL29 (Isle of Wight)

Turn right out of the car park and walk down through the village past the Wight Mouse Inn to St Andrew's Church. Turn left onto the main road, then almost immediately right into The Terrace, signposted 'pedestrians to Blackgang'. Bear left at Brickhill Lodge onto the coastal path bridleway, which opens out near the top to give some fine sea views. Turn right as the coastal path rejoins the main road, and follow the wide left-hand grass verge past the Blackgang Chine roundabout **A**.

Cross over here and continue for 200 yds to a stile in the hedge on your right. Nip over the stile and follow the signposted coastal path as it bears left around the edge of a grassy field to a second stile. Cross this one, too, and continue along the narrow path until a third stile leads you out onto the main road at the car park for St Catherine's Oratory. *From here, a well-signposted 550 yd diversion will lead you up to the Oratory, and down again by the same route.*

Turn right through the car park to continue your walk. There's usually a refreshment caravan here, offering hot drinks and soup as well as a good selection of home-made cakes, biscuits and Chale Farm ice creams. Follow the coastal path up a short flight of steps as it leaves the car park and turns left along the clifftop. After 50 yds cross the stile on your

Chale and Niton WALK 9 **49**

left and head across the open field back to the main road. Turn right, and follow the wide grass verge for 100 yds.

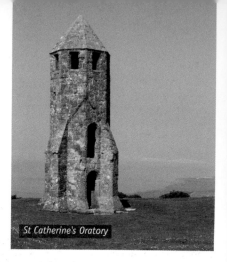
St Catherine's Oratory

Cross over the road, and turn left along bridleway NT52 towards Niton **B**. After 100 yds the bridleway turns off to the right; this is fast, easy walking along a delightful grassy track with sweeping sea views. Simply follow the wire fence on your left until the track drops between hedges to rejoin the main road just west of Niton **C**.

Turn left along the grass verge and continue onto the pavement as it bears left through Niton village. Soon you'll reach the church of St John the Baptist on your left; turn left here to begin the climb up Pan Lane towards St Catherine's Hill. Your way continues straight ahead onto bridleway NT53 as it follows Bury Lane through a tunnel of low trees, with glimpses of the Pepperpot on your left-hand side.

At the T-junction with Crocker Lane **D** you'll see Hoy's Monument sticking above the trees on the skyline straight ahead. Turn left here, and follow this lovely green path as it leads you around the valley to a small metal gate. Beyond the gate the path climbs gently across the open down, with far-reaching views on your right.

Keep ahead through a wicket gate to a pair of waymarked wooden gateposts on the crest of the hill **E**.

Here another glorious vista carries your eye all the way along the south coast of the island as far as Tennyson Down and the Needles. Bear right between the gateposts, and follow the lane as it drops through a metal field gate and bears steadily left, continuing as a narrow path across rough ground and heading directly towards Chale church tower. Now the path drops to a wicket gate and turns left along a track through Chale Farm. Turn right at the junction with Upper House Lane and follow it down to the B3399. Zigzag left and right across the road to return to your car. ■

Two towers stand sentinel over St Catherine's Down. To the south, the 14th-century St Catherine's Uratory – known locally as the **Pepperpot** – is Britain's second oldest lighthouse. One mile farther north, Hoy's Monument commemorates a visit by Tsar Nicholas I in 1814.

? *Why is there a lychgate at Niton church?*

Mottistone and the coast

- ■ Varied walking
- ■ standing stone
- ■ National Trust gardens
- ■ Chilton Farm ices

This varied walk follows byways, field and forest paths as it climbs steadily up to the halfway point at Long Stone. After dropping back through the woods to Mottistone Manor with its attractive gardens, a brisk walk down Ridget Lane prepares you for the final stretch along the cliff top coastal path.

walk 10

The Long Stone

walk 10

START Chilton Chine

DISTANCE 3¾ miles (6km)

TIME 2 hours

PARKING Small car park at the start

ROUTE FEATURES This route climbs almost 350 ft from the coast to the Long Stone. There are seven stiles, and some sections may be muddy. *Please lead dogs through fields beyond Strawberry Lane*

GPS WAYPOINTS

 SZ 409 822
Ⓐ SZ 414 834
Ⓑ SZ 412 840
Ⓒ SZ 405 837
Ⓓ SZ 401 825

PUBLIC TRANSPORT Bus services to Mottistone from Newport, Yarmouth and Freshwater (0871 200 2233)

REFRESHMENTS Mottistone Manor tea garden; Isle of Wight Pearl coffee shop; ice creams at Chilton Farm

PUBLIC TOILETS None

ORDNANCE SURVEY MAPS Explorer OL29 (Isle of Wight)

Cross the road from the car park and follow footpath BS71 towards Chilton Green. Beyond the green-painted chalets the track bears right, then left, to Chilton Green. Fork left onto the road at Chilton Farm; then, 150 yds farther on, fork right onto the byway to-wards Brighstone. The tree-shaded track bears left, then climbs steadily to the T-junction at Pitt Place Ⓐ.

Turn right onto the road and continue for 220 yds to the house at Grammar's Hill; *take care here, as there's no pavement on this section*. Turn left just beyond the house onto the narrow footpath BS67 towards Lynch Lane, climb up through a low tunnel of trees, and cross the stile into a conifer plantation. At first the path follows the left-hand edge of the plantation, before bearing away to the right and climbing deeper into the woods. One hundred yards farther on, your path meets a wider track at a lonely waymark post. Bear left here, and climb steeply for a short distance to a broader level section that contours gently around to the right.

Soon the path drops gently through an area of young conifers, bears to the left, and leaves the plantation at a stile. There are sea views here, as well as a bench seat that offers a welcome refreshment break. Beyond the stile, follow the bare track across an open field to a

Mottistone Manor

second stile that leads out onto Strawberry Lane **B**.

Turn right along the lane, follow it for 100 yds, then swing left onto footpath BS84 at a wooden gate that leads into the National Trust's Mottistone estate. Continue through a wicket gate and across the grazing fields to the Long Stone. Curiously enough there are two stones here – all that remains of the 4,000-year-old Neolithic burial chamber that was one of the oldest man-made structures on the island.

A **manor house** has stood at Mottistone since the time of Domesday, though the present buildings date from the 16th and 17th centuries. A landslide engulfed the rear of the property in 1703, and it wasn't until the 1920s that John Seely – later Lord Mottistone – had the earth carted away as part of an extensive renovation programme. Lord Mottistone bequeathed the house and its 650-acre (236ha) estate to the National Trust in 1963.

? *How often do they cut the grass in Mottistone churchyard?*

Directly beside the Long Stone, turn left onto the narrow sunken path that drops down through a patch of gorse, bracken and young oak. Continue through a kissing-gate as a forest track crosses your route; drop down a few rough steps, then bear right along the indistinct path that winds through the woodlands surrounding Mottistone Manor. Bear left when you reach a more confident sunken track

★ Just across Chilton Chine from the start of this walk, **Isle of Wight Pearl** offers the UK's widest range of pearl jewellery under a single roof. You'll also find a selection of contemporary gold and silver, as well as a range of craft materials at Olly's Beadery. The on-site Smuggler's coffee shop enjoys spectacular views from this glorious cliff top location.

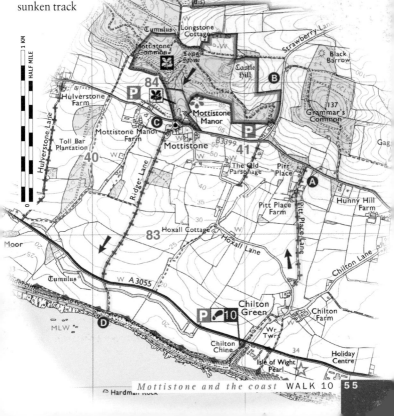

at the *Long Stone* signpost, and follow it down through the trees to the B3399 **C**.

Mottistone, Church of St Peter & St Paul

Turn left past the entrance to Mottistone Manor, then right into Church Lane. Continue past the church into Ridget Lane and follow the lane as it bears left, leaves the tarmac behind, and heads straight for the coast. A stretch of fast, easy walking brings you to the Military Road; cross over, jump the stile opposite and join footpath BS75 for the final link with the coastal path.

Jump the next stile too, and follow the wire fence on your right. Now you can smell the sea, and a final stile brings you, at last, to the coastal path **D**.

Turn left, and follow the path along the top of these crumbling southern cliffs, taking note of any signposted diversions. *Once again care is needed, as you're only a few feet from the edge on this section.* Now you can see the whitewashed buildings at Isle of Wight Pearl, just beyond Chilton Chine – and, to your left, you should be able to pick out most of the circular route that you've followed since leaving your car.

Just short of Isle of Wight Pearl, turn left along the top of the chine for the short distance back to the car park.

Freshwater and Tennyson Down

■ Superb views   ■ popular beach

■ famous landmark   ■ unique thatched church

This varied route begins with dramatic coastal landscapes, then drops into Freshwater Bay for a change of scene. After continuing through Afton Marsh nature reserve, a woodland stroll along the back of the Downs completes the loop. For a longer walk, the route can easily be combined with Walk 7.

walk 11

Tennyson's monument

walk 11

START National Trust car park at the top of Highdown Lane

DISTANCE 3¾ miles (6km)

TIME 2 hours

PARKING NT car park

ROUTE FEATURES The gradients on this walk are long and steady, rather than steep. *Please take particular care near unfenced cliff edges especially with children.* Dogs should be led near grazing animals on the Down, and through Afton Marsh nature reserve

GPS WAYPOINTS

🔾 SZ 324 855
Ⓐ SZ 319 853
Ⓑ SZ 324 853
Ⓒ SZ 345 858
Ⓓ SZ 342 860

PUBLIC TRANSPORT Bus services to Freshwater from Yarmouth and Newport (0871 200 2233)

REFRESHMENTS Freshwater Bay Tea Rooms; Albion Hotel; Cameron Tearoom at Dimbola Lodge

PUBLIC TOILETS Gate Lane, Freshwater Bay

ORDNANCE SURVEY MAPS Explorer OL29 (Isle of Wight)

🔾 Set off as if to leave the car park by road, then turn immediately left past a low wooden barrier into the National Trust's Tennyson Down estate. Follow the lightly wooded green lane for nearly ½ mile until you reach a replica of the old Nodes Beacon standing prominently beside a stile at a footpath 'cross roads' Ⓐ.

Double back to your left at the beacon, now following the coastal footpath as it heads out through some gorse bushes towards the Tennyson Memorial on the summit of the Down Ⓑ. There are bench seats around the memorial, which is a natural focus for walkers. From here, a breathtaking panorama encompasses a wide sweep along the island's south coast from St Catherine's, as well as Hurst Castle, the Solent and the New Forest in the north. *But do not let any of that distract you from the fact that the memorial is scarcely 25 yds from the cliff edge, with a 480-ft drop to the beach below.*

Continue along the scant downland path past the memorial towards Freshwater Bay, keeping about 50 yds from the cliff edge. There's a kissing-gate where you leave the Down. Fork left here, following the well-trodden grassy path down to a small wooden gate, then turn left to the junction with Gate Lane **C**.

> In addition to Tennyson Down, the National Trust now owns much of the **West Wight** peninsula, including West High Down and Headon Warren. The area is part of the chalk ridge that forms the island's backbone – and once linked the island to Ballard Down near Swanage in Dorset. The natural woodland was cleared for grazing during the Stone Age, and the Downs now contain some of Britain's finest chalk grassland.

Turn right at the end, towards the beach; then, after 100 yds, turn left at the tearooms into Coastguard Lane. Pass

the Cameron Tearoom and
continue as the gravelled road
merges into a country path and
goes through a waymarked

? *What was the date of Tennyson's death?*

kissing-gate into Afton Marsh local nature reserve. A second kissing-gate
leads down six steps and across a boardwalk to a fork in the path; keep
left, and continue out onto Blackbridge Road. *There's no pavement on
this section, so do watch out for the occasional car as you turn left along
the road* as far as the T-junction opposite St Agnes' Church **D**.

This charming little building is the only thatched church on the island
and looks much older than it really is. Much of the building material was
recovered from a derelict old farmhouse, and a large stone near the
vestry door carries the date 1694. Yet, despite this, the church was

Freshwater Bay

actually built in 1908 to replace the former mission church or 'iron room' that stood nearby. The land was given by the Tennyson family.

Zigzag left and right across the main road and continue through a kissing-gate up footpath F46 towards Tennyson Down and the Needles. The path runs between hedges to a waymarked wicket gate, then follows the edge of an open field beside the hedge on your right-hand side. After 200 yds, a signpost points your way to the right, through a field gate onto a delightful tree-shaded green lane. Keep left when the path divides at a waymark post and National Trust marker stone, and continue until you reach a fork 100 yds beyond the worked-out quarry on your left. Keep left here, and climb gently through the low tunnel of trees that leads you through a kissing-gate to a small grassy clearing, where you drop down into the car park where your walk began. ∎

Newchurch

- Historic church
- young woodlands
- old railway path
- nature trail

walk 12

The walk drops steeply downhill from Newchurch and turns briefly east along the old railway, now part of the national cycle network. From here it turns north to follow the Bembridge Trail between Knighton and Kern Farm, before dropping down into Alverstone village. A final section along the old railway and Newchurch Parish Nature Trail completes the loop.

Newchurch & Pointer Inn

walk 12

START School Lane car park

DISTANCE 4 miles (6.4km)

TIME 2 hours

PARKING At the start

ROUTE FEATURES Generally easy walking, with only a few stiles, though the woodland sections may be muddy. Please lead dogs through the churchyard and along the short sections of road, as well as on the Bembridge Trail and through the newly planted woodland

GPS WAYPOINTS

- 📷 SZ 561 854
- **Ⓐ** SZ 559 859
- **Ⓑ** SZ 566 868
- **Ⓒ** SZ 578 866
- **Ⓓ** SZ 577 855

PUBLIC TRANSPORT Limited bus service from Newport and Shanklin (0871 200 2233)

REFRESHMENTS Pointer Inn: Gales ales, home-made food, family garden

PUBLIC TOILETS None

ORDNANCE SURVEY MAPS Explorer OL29 (Isle of Wight)

📷 Turn right out of the car park, then right again past the Pointer Inn. Dodge to your right through the church gates and continue to a small iron gate at the corner of the churchyard. Follow the narrow stepped path steeply downhill, and turn left at the bottom onto a tree-shaded lane. Rejoin the road, turn right, and follow it to Newchurch Crossing **Ⓐ**. *Take care here, as there's no pavement and the road is quite narrow.*

Turn right onto the old railway, now part of the Sustrans national cycle network. After 550 yds turn left onto the signposted bridleway towards Knighton, a pleasant dirt track with good downland views. Continue onto Lower Knighton Lane, and keep straight on at the next junction towards Newport and Ryde. Pass Knighton Farm, where the Bembridge Trail swings in from the left, and keep going until the road bears gently left.

Turn right here onto bridleway NC45 towards Knighton Waterworks and Alverstone **Ⓑ**. The lane winds through a small group of cottages, then climbs gently through light mixed woodland until a blue waymark at Harts Ash Farm points your way to the right. Now the trail drops through a tree-shaded sunken way; bear left at the end of this hollow, signposted towards Kern. The sandy track winds onwards, crosses the access road to Knighton

Newchurch WALK 12 **63**

sandpit, and comes to a four-way signpost at a byway crossroads.

Continue through the field gate straight ahead, following the Bembridge Trail towards Kern and Alverstone. The grassy track bears to the left beside open fields, with a hedge on your left and wide views to the right. Another gate leads you through a short section shaded by trees and high gorse, until the path climbs gently from a third gate to the buildings at Kern Farm **C**.

> ***** The 11-mile **Bembridge Trail** is one of eight inland routes linking the interior of the island with the coastal path. Starting from Shide on the outskirts of Newport, the trail threads its way through woods and downland scenery to Nunwell House and the historic town of Brading (see *Walk 6*). The route continues past Bembridge windmill (*Walk 15*) to reach the mouth of the River Yar at Bembridge.

Double back to your right through the farm gate, following the bridleway towards Alverstone as it swings

> **?** *What does the name 'Alverstone' mean?*

left onto a small country lane. Stick with the lane as it swings back to the right and drops gently down to the beautifully renovated buildings at Chiddle's Farm. Nip over the stile ahead of you and continue along the right-hand field edge, following the footpath towards Alverstone and Knighton. Continue over the stile in the far corner of the field until, after 70 yds, the path turns left into Alverstone. Turn right through the village as far as the old railway crossing **D** with its white painted gates, where the old station house still stands beside the national cycleway.

Turn right along the cycleway and follow it to a four-way signpost 450 yds farther on. Turn left here over a little footbridge onto footpath NC11 towards Newchurch, continuing through a narrow belt of trees and a kissing-gate. Cross an open field to a second kissing-gate, then immediately fork right through the open woodland to a third kissing-

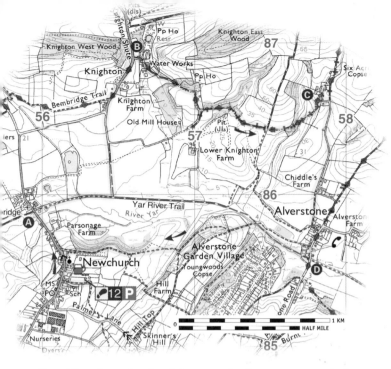

gate. Now follow the enclosed path between wire fences to a waymarked wooden wicket gate; turn right here, cross a small plank bridge, and climb gently up through young woodland beside the wire fence on your right. Bear left at the top, following footpath NC11 along the top of the plantation.

As the path approaches Newchurch it runs beside All Saints graveyard wall; keep the wall on your left, then go through an opening and up three steps into the field behind the church. Turn right along the tarmac path, then left at the end to retrace your steps past the Pointer and back to the car park.

Newchurch, Garlic Shop

Carisbrooke and its castle

- Famous castle
- downland views
- waterside causeway
- varied scenery

walk 13

There are plenty of castle views along this route, which pushes out to the west of Carisbrooke along farm tracks and quiet green lanes. A steep climb brings you up to the Tennyson Trail, and the walk loops back through Carisbrooke village before closing with a dramatic final section around the castle ramparts.

Carisbrooke Castle ramparts

walk 13

START Carisbrooke Priory car park

DISTANCE 4¼ miles (6.8km)

TIME 2 hours

PARKING At the start

ROUTE FEATURES Please lead your dog through the farms and along White Lane, as well as in Carisbrooke village

GPS WAYPOINTS
SZ 489 875
Ⓐ SZ 474 869
Ⓑ SZ 468 874
Ⓒ SZ 485 882

PUBLIC TRANSPORT Bus connections from all the main Island towns (0871 200 2233)

REFRESHMENTS The Eight Bells: Free house, all day menu, families welcome, dining area, garden and play area; The Waverley: Free house, bar food, garden

PUBLIC TOILETS Carisbrooke High Street

ORDNANCE SURVEY MAPS Explorer OL29 (Isle of Wight)

Face the castle, turn left along the wide grass verge, and fork right into Froglands Lane. The road bears away to the right at the bottom of the hill, but your way lies straight ahead along the footpath that follows the gravelled track towards Froglands Farm. Pass the picturesque farm buildings on your left and follow the tree-shaded track as it bears right past a bridleway signpost and pulls out into open countryside. There are glorious views of Bowcombe Down on your right here, before the path bears to the right and drops down an old sunken way through a tunnel of trees. Pass the junction with footpath N104, and continue for 170 yds to a fork in the path Ⓐ.

Turn left here onto an attractive green lane that runs between hedges to a T-junction at Bowcombe Farm. Turn right, and follow the byway as it winds past the farm buildings and climbs gently up to the busy Bowcombe Road. Cross over, turn right, and follow the pavement for 250 yds before turning left onto bridleway N127 towards White Lane and the Tennyson Trail. The tree-shaded track climbs steeply to a metal field gate and, a few paces farther on, you'll reach a crossroads with the Tennyson Trail Ⓑ. It's a good place to stop

> **?** *Who was Rev William James Stobart?*

Carisbrooke, Lukely Brook

for a breather, as well as to admire the view across the valley towards Garstons Down.

Turn right onto the Tennyson Trail, and follow the rough farm road that leads you down into Carisbrooke village. Much of this section is hemmed in by trees, but there are occasional views of the castle to your right and, in late summer, a profusion of butterflies will keep you company on the road. The trail drops gently at first, then more steeply as you approach the outskirts of Carisbrooke and reach the junction with a quiet residential road. Turn left, then bear right into High Street; cross over, and follow the pavement on the left-hand side of the road. Pass The Waverley, keep straight on at the mini-roundabout, and continue through St Mary's churchyard to the south door of this imposing church.

Drop down the steps immediately opposite the church, cross the road, and turn into Castle Street **C**. Continue along the charming causeway beside the Lukely Brook; then, 50 yds farther on, swing left up Castle Lane and follow it to the junction with the castle access road. Cross over, take the footpath directly ahead of you, and follow it as it skulks through the trees at the foot of the castle mound. Turn right after 25 yds up a flight of slippery stone steps, then bear left up a second flight that leads you up onto the castle ramparts.

Bear left, and continue along the ramparts with the castle walls on your right. Follow the walls around a sharp right-hand bend; then, just before the next bend, turn sharp left onto the waymarked footpath that leads steeply down off the castle mound. At the foot of the slope the narrow path bears right and runs across the little valley to meet your outward route at Froglands Lane. Turn left, and retrace your outward steps for the short way back to your car.

Carisbrooke Castle stands in a commanding position close to the centre of the island, and the site was probably fortified in both Roman and Saxon times. The present castle was founded by the Normans, and development continued right through to the Tudor period. Later, King Charles I was held prisoner at Carisbrooke during the Civil War – but nowadays, children are more likely to be fascinated by the donkeys that power the **giant waterwheel** beside the castle's well.

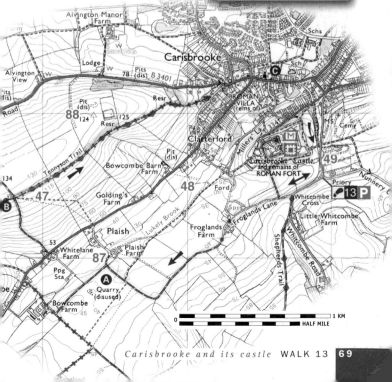

The western Yar

■ **Yar Swing Bridge**
■ **historic castle**
■ **bird watching**
■ **old railway path**

There are great river views as the walk strikes out down the old railway path along the eastern shore of the River Yar. After crossing the causeway and climbing to the picturesque Red Lion beside All Saints' Church, the return journey along country paths is largely out of sight of the river.

Moored boats at Yarmouth Harbour

walk 14

START River Road car park

DISTANCE 3¾ miles (6km)

TIME 2 hours

PARKING Pay and Display car park at the start

ROUTE FEATURES Active wheelchair users can enjoy the nicely surfaced outward route along the old Freshwater railway line. The return loop includes eight stiles, and follows well-signposted rural paths that may be muddy

GPS WAYPOINTS

- 📷 SZ 353 896
- Ⓐ SZ 356 891
- Ⓑ SZ 352 879
- Ⓒ SZ 348 871
- Ⓓ SZ 347 896

PUBLIC TRANSPORT Bus connections from all the main Island towns (0871 200 2233). Wightlink ferry service from Lymington (0871 376 1000)

REFRESHMENTS The Red Lion, Freshwater. Yarmouth: Good selection of cafés and pubs

PUBLIC TOILETS Bridge Road, Yarmouth

PLAY AREA None

ORDNANCE SURVEY MAPS Explorer OL29 (Isle of Wight)

✳ The Yar Valley has been settled since prehistoric times and contains several important **archaeological sites**. The medieval town of Yarmouth was listed as Eremue in *Domesday Book* and the castle, completed in 1547, was garrisoned during the Civil War. A small ferry carried travellers across the estuary until the old Yar bridge was built in 1863; it was replaced by the present bridge in 1987.

📷 Turn right out of the main car park entrance, pass the primary school, and turn right into Mill Road. As the road turns left into Station Road, continue along the signposted footpath towards Freshwater and Broad Lane. Bear right along the edge of the river, and through a wicket gate onto the old railway path Ⓐ towards The Causeway and Freshwater.

This well-engineered route will carry you all the way south to The Causeway.

Ⓑ Footpath F24 branches off towards Wilmingham Lane as you reach Backet's Plantation. Then, as the old line approaches The Causeway, a bench seat near the old landing stage makes a good spot to stop for a few minutes to watch the birds, or simply to enjoy the river views.

Turn right over The Causeway Ⓒ, pass the wartime pill-box on your left, and climb the short hill to the church and the Red Lion pub. Directly in front of the church turn right onto the Freshwater Way, which will carry you all the way back to Yarmouth. The narrow path runs beside the churchyard to a stile, then continues briefly between wire fences with fields on each side.

A second stile leads you out onto a tarmac lane; keep straight on here, with a row of bungalows on your left and views to the river on your right. The lane continues to a fork at Kings Manor Farm. Follow the Freshwater Way as it dodges to the left over a smart double stile and plank bridge and bears to the right along a well-signposted route behind the farm buildings. Cross the next stile, too, and continue through a small plantation.

Beyond this little wood, the path bears left through a kissing-gate and leads you along a muddy farm track that climbs gently over a low summit with views across the river towards Yarmouth on your right. Continue through a small oakwood as the Freshwater Way veers to the right and carries you across two sets of stiles and plank bridges in quick succession.

The Causeway

Bear left here, climbing beside the woodland edge until the signposted path strikes out beside a wire fence separating two fields. Go over the stile at the top of another low hill and follow the muddy path as it winds through Saltern Wood to meet

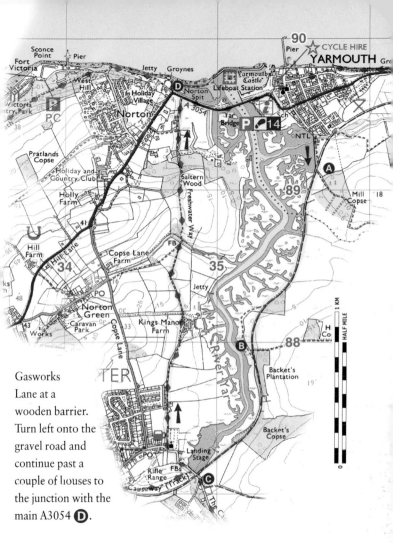

Gasworks
Lane at a
wooden barrier.
Turn left onto the
gravel road and
continue past a
couple of houses to
the junction with the
main A3054 **D**.

Turn right, following the roadside
pavement over the harbour bridge and
past the Yarmouth Sailing Club to the
mini-roundabout. Now, simply bear
right to return to your car. ■

> **?** *When did Isle of
> Wight Council
> attain the national
> rights-of-way target?*

Around Bembridge

walk 15

■ Cliff walking   ■ shady woodlands
■ historic windmill   ■ sea views

*This route encircles the little town of Bembridge.
Starting from the lifeboat station, the walk cuts behind
the Bembridge Coast Hotel to emerge on the cliff path.
There are good views across Whitecliff Bay here, before
turning inland through the woods to Bembridge
Windmill. A further woodland stretch precedes a gentle
finish along quiet private roads.*

Whitecliff Bay

walk 15

START Lane End car park

DISTANCE 4¼ miles (6.8km)

TIME 2 hours

PARKING Pay and Display car park at the start

ROUTE FEATURES Generally easy walking, *but do take care where the path runs close to the clifftops*

GPS WAYPOINTS

　　 SZ 656 880
Ⓐ SZ 655 873
Ⓑ SZ 642 864
Ⓒ SZ 638 872
Ⓓ SZ 645 885

PUBLIC TRANSPORT Buses from Ryde, Newport and Sandown (0871 200 2233)

REFRESHMENTS Crab and Lobster, Pilot Boat Inn, Toll Gate café, Lifeboat View café

PUBLIC TOILETS At the start, also opposite the Pilot Boat Inn. (No toilets at Bembridge Windmill)

ORDNANCE SURVEY MAPS Explorer OL29 (Isle of Wight)

Face the sea and turn right along the coastal path B42, continuing as it turns right at the end of the small green. Cross the road at the Bembridge Coast Hotel and continue straight down the narrow footpath. Turn left at the end, following the coast path along Foreland Farm Lane. Turn right at the end into Howgate Road, then left into Beachfield Road, and continue along the coastal path as it bears right past the Coastguard Station and the Crab and Lobster pub Ⓐ.

Now the narrow path winds along the top of the crumbling cliffs, with glorious views across Whitecliff Bay. At length, you reach the red brick buildings of the Bembridge Environmental Field Study Centre. Pass the climbing tower, and continue for 100 yds to a signpost and interpretation panel on your right Ⓑ.

Beyond Whitecliff Bay, the **Yarborough memorial** stands out clearly on the top of Culver Down. It was erected by public subscription in memory of Charles Anderson Pelham, Earl of Yarborough, whose 'benevolence and kindness of heart endeared him to all who knew him'. The Earl, who lived at Appuldurcombe House near Wroxall *(see Walks 3 and 17)*, was a keen sailor and first Commodore of the Royal Yacht Squadron. He died aboard his yacht *Kestrel* in September 1846.

Bembridge, Crab & Lobster pub

Turn right here, following the waymarked route around the Centre buildings and up the woodland track to the junction with Hillway Road. Turn left, walk down the hill for 100 yds, then turn right along the signposted footpath BB22 to Steyne Wood and Bembridge Windmill. Two stiles punctuate the woodland route as the path crosses Sandown Road. Then, 100 yds farther on, bear right **C** onto the attractive bridleway that climbs steadily to Bembridge Windmill.

Continue past the mill and keep straight on at the road junction. *Take care here, because there's no pavement for most of the next 500 yds.* Two hundred yards beyond Grange Gardens, turn left onto footpath BB3, signposted towards The Point. The path drops into the woods, then swings to the right and follows a wooden boardwalk to reach the gravelled lane leading to the Pilot Boat Inn. (*From here, the Toll Gate Café is just around the corner on your left.*) Cross the road from the pub, and follow the signposted coastal path up a private road until you reach a broad gravelled track **D**.

Yar Trail milestone

Cross the gravelled track and follow the signposted coastal path until it meets Love Lane at a sharp bend. Zigzag left and right onto the

? Who gave Bembridge Windmill to the National Trust?

road, and follow the signposted route until it merges with bridleway BB35. Keep straight along the bridleway as it crosses Swains Road and continue along Swains Lane to the junction with Lane End Road. Turn left here, for the last 300 yds back to the lifeboat station. ■

Bembridge windmill

Beside the Medina

- Riverside walk
- all-weather path
- nature reserve
- bus ride

This level walk leaves Cowes along residential roads and joins the old railway cycle path on the edge of town. There are plenty of river views and, in a couple of places, you can walk right down to the water's edge. After crossing Dodnor Creek nature reserve the walk runs beside Newport harbour as it threads its way into the town centre.

walk 16

Bargeman's Rest, Newport

walk 16

START Red Funnel ferry terminal, Cowes

DISTANCE 4½ miles (7.2km)

TIME 2½ hours

PARKING Cowes: Denmark Road Pay and Display car park, 75 yds from bus station

ROUTE FEATURES The surface of this old railway cycle route is ideal for more adventurous wheelchair users. Fouling by dogs is an offence

GPS WAYPOINTS

  SZ 496 961
  Ⓐ SZ 498 947
  Ⓑ SZ 500 937
  Ⓒ SZ 503 916
  Ⓓ SZ 500 901

PUBLIC TRANSPORT High-speed ferry service from Southampton (0844 844 9988). A frequent bus service links Newport with Cowes (0871 200 2233)

REFRESHMENTS Plenty in Newport and Cowes, no refreshment facilities in between the two towns

PUBLIC TOILETS Cowes: Denmark Road; Newport: South Street (next to bus station)

ORDNANCE SURVEY MAPS Explorer OL29 (Isle of Wight)

Leave the ferry terminal under the arch and turn left into High Street. Pass the Carvel Lane bus station just off High Street on your right and bear left into the pedestrianised area. Continue into Shooters Hill and bear left at the top into Birmingham Road, signposted towards the floating bridge. Zigzag right and left at the Duke of York into York Street and keep going over the staggered crossroads into Pelham Road. Take the first turning right into South Road, climb the short hill, and turn left at the top into Arctic Road. Continue past the UK Sailing Academy until, at the very end of the road, you zigzag right and left onto the signposted cycle path towards Newport Ⓐ.

The path edges its way clear of industrial Cowes through a tunnel of oak, ash and birch. Just beyond the chimneys of Cowes Power Station on the far bank, look out for attractive views down the small creek on your left. So far there's been little to betray the path's railway ancestry but, a short way past the signposted footpath CS33 to Northwood on your right, you'll come to the broken remains of an iron and timber bridge Ⓑ, with trees growing up through the old road decking.

There are more glimpses of colourful moored sailing craft and, half-hidden in the trees on the far bank, look out for the Victorian pinnacles of St Mildred's Church in

? *What's the name of the derelict old paddle-steamer halfway along the far bank? (You'll need your binoculars for this one.)*

Whippingham. The original church was extravagantly rebuilt in the mid-19th century, and used by the Royal family during their stays at nearby Osborne House. The views gradually open out around Pinkmead, and soon you'll spot the old paddle-steamer slowly rusting away near the marina on the far bank.

✳ This walk makes a great day out from **Southampton** using the Red Jet ferry. You'll have plenty of time to explore Cowes and Newport, and there are eight buses an hour (four on Sundays) to get you back to the start. If you're already on the Island, you might prefer to park in Newport and catch the bus to the start – that way, your car will be waiting for you at the end.

Royal Yacht Squadron, Cowes

Cross Stag Lane **C**, and the newly restored viaduct across Dodnor Creek nature reserve. The path now climbs to a level crossing with Dodnor Lane, in place of the bridge that originally carried the road above the railway. A little farther on, look out for wild birds feeding on the intertidal mudflats, oblivious to the modern industrial buildings that start to huddle round as you approach the northern outskirts of Newport.

Now you're almost at the white-painted gates that mark the end of the cycle path **D**. Keep straight on at the roundabout, and continue to the phone box on the corner of Hurstake Road. Turn left here, drop down to the T-junction and turn right. Follow the road past the harbour and the Bargeman's Rest, and continue under the flyover to the Quay Arts Centre at the junction with Sea Street. Turn right, then left at the T-junction, and head up Holyrood Street towards St Thomas's Church tower in the centre of town. Cross High Street, and continue through St Thomas Square into Pyle Street, where the car park is just a few yards away on your right. *Alternatively, keep straight on down Town Lane to reach the bus station in South Street.* ■

Dodnor Creek was dammed in the 1790s to power a proposed tide mill. Now a local **nature reserve**, the creek is rich in birdlife and you might see reed and sedge warblers as well as coot, moorhen and swans. The reserve stretches up towards the ancient woodlands of Dickson's Copse, where unusual butterflies flutter above the bluebells, primroses and orchids in the clearings.

Cowes High Street

Godshill and Appuldurcombe

- Famous church
- model village
- cream teas
- ruined house

After threading its way through Godshill village the walk heads south over the Worsley Trail to Gat Cliff. From here, it's an unremitting climb to the radio station high on Stenbury Down, where the route veers north and drops back down into rural farmland. The return leg makes its way back to Godshill past the brooding remains of Appuldurcombe House.

Appuldurcombe House

walk 17

START The Old Smithy car park, Godshill

DISTANCE 5 miles (8km)

TIME 2½ hours

PARKING At the start

ROUTE FEATURES This strenuous walk climbs 600 ft to Stenbury Down. Some stiles, and the route may be muddy. *Please lead dogs through Godshill village, and near grazing animals*

GPS WAYPOINTS

📷 SZ 531 816
🅐 SZ 526 817
🅑 SZ 526 808
🅒 SZ 533 805
🅓 SZ 539 793
🅔 SZ 545 792
🅕 SZ 543 801
🅖 SZ 540 807

PUBLIC TRANSPORT Bus services from Newport, Ryde, Sandown, Shanklin and Ventnor
(0871 200 2233)

REFRESHMENTS Tea gardens in Godshill village; The Griffin, The Cask & Taverners; Aviary café, Appuldurcombe

PUBLIC TOILETS At start, and at Appuldurcombe House

ORDNANCE SURVEY MAPS Explorer OL29 (Isle of Wight)

👣 Turn right out of the car park, walk up the High Street, and continue around the right-hand bend to the Post Office. Cross over, turn left, and walk up Church Hollow towards the church. At the top of the hill you'll find the classic chocolate-box view of All Saints church tower rising above the thatched cottages on your right.

🅐 Turn left here and follow the lane south. Pass a junction on your left and then, 100 yds farther on, fork left into Sheepwash Lane. Continue past Sainham Farm to an unsignposted gap in the left-hand hedge, almost at the brow of the hill 🅑.

> ✳ The influential Worsley family lived at **Appuldurcombe House** for three centuries. James Worsley had been a page to Henry VII; he was later knighted by Henry VIII and awarded a plethora of civil and military posts on the island. The family were shrewd political operators, married well, and successive generations continued to find Royal favour. They filled Appuldurcombe with pictures and important classical antiquities, but the collection was largely dispersed after the house was sold in 1855.

Turn hard left through the gap, and follow the path between newly planted saplings towards the left-hand corner of the woods ahead. Bear right along the woodland edge path and continue through the gates behind Sainham

Farm to a stile on your right. Bear right over the stile onto footpath GL58, following the Worsley Trail towards Stenbury Down. The well-made track climbs to a mobile phone mast on your left, continues through a large steel gate, and bears right for the climb towards Gat Cliff. Soon a stile carries you through a

Godshill Model Village, Godshill church

patch of woodland to a second stile and a parting of the ways **C**.

Turn hard right here, and follow bridleway GL49 through a large metal gate towards Stenbury Down and Ventnor. Now a series of small gates leads you along the edge of an open field, past a turning on the right, and up the lightly wooded hill. Continue as the path swings to the left around the back of a disused chalk pit, and follow the hedge on your left-hand side towards the far radio station on Stenbury Down.

There are splendid views all along this section, and you can take in St Catherine's Oratory, Hoy's Monument and the south coast in one sweeping panorama. As you approach the transmitter, look out for a small metal gate on your left. Dodge through here, and join bridleway GL51 as it tracks the service road towards the mast, signposted to Week Down and Ventnor.

Beyond the radio station **D**, follow the service road as it sweeps around to the left and plunges down to meet Rew Lane opposite Bumble's Cottage **E**.

How close can you park to the radio station on Stenbury Down?

Turn left here; then, as the road veers to the right, keep straight on past Span Lodge along footpath GL47 towards Appuldurcombe House. Go through a gate and continue through the fields to Appuldurcombe, where a stile leads you along the iron boundary railings with excellent views of the house.

Sir Robert Worsley began building the present house in 1701 on the site of an earlier Tudor mansion, but the project was a constant financial drain and was still unfinished when he died. His successor, Sir James Worsley, showed no interest in the house and it was left to his grandson,

Sir Richard Worsley, to complete the building in the late 18th century. Sir Richard chose 'Capability' Brown to landscape the park, and employed Thomas Chippendale to produce his furniture.

* **Godshill** village is a piece of Olde England wrapped up in pretty paper and sold back to you – but, for all that, the place is still worth a visit. Attractions like the cider barn, the toy museum and the model village all vie for your attention on the High Street, while **one of England's most photographed views** lies tucked away at the top of Church Hollow. Cream teas are mandatory.

Further improvements were made to Appuldurcombe in the early 19th century before the Worsleys sold the estate in 1855. The new owner had planned to convert the house into a hotel, but the project came to nothing and Appuldurcombe was used for a time as a boys' school. The building later became a temporary refuge for French Benedictine monks, but from 1909 it lay empty. Its slow decline was hastened by damage caused during the Second World War, and by the 1950s the derelict house narrowly escaped demolition. Now it is in the care of English Heritage, the partly restored building is an alluring blend of stately home and ruined shell. Simply follow the railings and stone wall around to the left, until you reach the car park **F** at the entrance to Appuldurcombe House and the Isle of Wight Owl and Falconry Centre *(mentioned in Walk 3)*.

Zigzag left and right past the car park, and join footpath GL47 towards Godshill. Continue northwards to the imposing Freemantle Gate at the edge of the park **G**.

Go through the gate and keep straight on along bridleway GL44 towards Godshill. From here it's plain sailing past Godshill Park House, where the track becomes a surfaced lane. Now keep straight on, all the way to the junction with Shanklin Road at Tyne Cottage. Turn left here, cross over the road, and follow the pavement back into Godshill and the car park where your walk began. ∎

Newtown Harbour and Hamstead Point

- Peaceful estuary
- coastal views
- varied walking
- waterside memorial

This figure-of-eight route follows the coastal path and the Hamstead Trail as it sets out through a wooded area of scattered housing towards the Newtown River. Then, you'll traverse marsh and wetland habitats before rounding Hamstead Point and heading back along gravelled tracks through a rural mosaic of open fields and mixed woodland.

walk 18

Newtown Harbour, walker on causeway

walk 18

START Horse & Groom pub, Ningwood

DISTANCE 5 miles (8km)

TIME 2½ hours

PARKING Please use the public car park next to the pub

ROUTE FEATURES Much of this remote route follows wide gravelled tracks, but *you'll also walk close to the water's edge and across low wooden causeways that may be submerged at high tide.* The walk includes ten stiles

GPS WAYPOINTS
- ✎ SZ 400 891
- Ⓐ SZ 401 904
- Ⓑ SZ 414 912
- Ⓒ SZ 409 919
- Ⓓ SZ 401 901

PUBLIC TRANSPORT Buses from Yarmouth and Newport (0871 200 2233)

REFRESHMENTS Horse & Groom, Ningwood: extensive all-day menu, garden and play area

PUBLIC TOILETS None

ORDNANCE SURVEY MAPS Explorer OL29 (Isle of Wight)

👢 Turn left out of the car park, follow the narrow verge beside the main road for 200 yds to Hamstead Drive, and turn left again up the signposted coastal path towards Hamstead. Follow the gently curving gravel road as it heads north past scattered houses and into Nunneys Wood. Cross the bridge at Ningwood Lake, and climb gently through the woods to a fork Ⓓ in the road near Pigeon Coo Farm. Keep straight on along the coastal path and Hamstead Trail to a second fork, 200 yds farther on Ⓐ.

> **?** *What's the latest posting time for letters on the Hamstead Trail?*

Fork right onto footpath S28 towards Yarmouth, still following the gravel road through mixed oak and conifer woodland.

Ningwood Lake

Gradually the trees slip behind you, and the road continues between hedges with occasional glimpses of the Newtown River up ahead. This is easy walking, but there are landmarks along the way; footpath S5 turns off to your left, and you pass Creek Farm Cottage before the road swings to the left and re-enters the woods. Look for river views on your right as the road makes a beeline for the jetty beyond the cream-washed Lower Hamstead Farm.

B Turn left 50 yds before you reach the jetty, following the coastal path and Hamstead Trail towards Bouldnor and Yarmouth. The enclosed path runs beside a dense hedge of blackthorn, gorse and bramble, then zigzags right and left, to run within inches of the water's edge. Now, a succession of low wooden causeways leads you away from the river and out into farmland.

Continue along the left-hand edge of the field as it rises beside the hedgerow trees on your left to give river views on the right-hand side. Just beyond the crest of this gentle rise, the path turns half left over a stile and heads diagonally across an open field. Nip over the stile in the far corner, and cross the long wooden causeway over a shallow arm of the Newtown River. From here, the path leads between thick hedges towards the sound of the surf on Hamstead Point.

Now the coastal path lives up to its name as it drops down a few steps and swings to the left along a grassy track right next to the beach **C**. As you round Hamstead Point, look out for the little stone memorial tucked in the bushes on your left; then, follow the coast path as it cuts inland up a stony, tree-shaded track that levels off and opens out with a field on the left-hand side. This is pleasant, gently rolling farmland with old trees in the hedgerows, but spare a backward glance for the seascape behind you.

There's a final glimpse across the Solent to Lymington as the coastal path crosses the signposted stiles at Hamstead Farm. Follow the gravel road as it winds past Grange Cottage and continues as footpath S30 towards the

Newport/Yarmouth road. The road bears right at the entrance to Hamstead Grange and, just here, there's a lovely vista across the Newtown River and the Solent towards Cowes. From here the road runs straight past Pennethorne Park Farm, rejoins your outward route just north of Pigeon Coo Farm **Ⓐ**, and comes to a fork 150 yds farther on.

Sailing on Newtown River

Ⓓ Turn right here onto the Hamstead Trail, still signposted towards the Newport/Yarmouth road. Pass the farm on your right, and carry on until you reach a letterbox at a fork in the track. Follow the Hamstead Trail around to the left, continue for 250 yds to a bend in the road, then turn left onto footpath S9 towards Ningwood. The path follows the woodland edge and comes to a stile; go over, and bear left across an open field. Cross two stiles in quick succession, then continue across a narrow field and over a little iron-railed footbridge into Nunneys Wood.

Leave the woods at a stile, still following the path towards Ningwood. Continue down the side of an open field until you reach a stile in the corner, quite close to the road. Nip across, back to the car park where your walk began. ■

> **✻** After more than 70 years, it's hard to decipher the worn lettering on the touching little memorial at **Hamstead Point**. The simple stone cross records the tragic deaths of three young men; the eldest, David Cox, was just 22 when he and his friend William Pollock were lost at sea off Hamstead Ledge in November 1932. Then, just 18 months later, Robin Cox suffered a similar fate.

Calbourne and Winkle Street

- ■ **Famous cottages**
- ■ **long views**
- ■ **forest trails**
- ■ **mapping heritage**

walk 19

The walk sets out along the Tennyson Trail for the climb onto Mottistone Down, then continues through Brighstone Forest and across farmland towards Calbourne and Winkle Street. The homeward stretch heads south along Lynch Lane. A steep climb over Brighstone Down leads you back to the Tennyson Trail for a downhill stroll to the finishing line.

Winkle Street

START Junction of Lynch Lane and Strawberry Lane, one mile north of Brighstone

DISTANCE 5½ miles (8.8km)

TIME 3 hours

PARKING At the start

ROUTE FEATURES *With two strenuous climbs, poor signposting and a dozen stiles, this walk is not for the faint-hearted. Please lead dogs through farmland*

GPS WAYPOINTS

- 🥾 SZ 420 845
- Ⓐ SZ 409 847
- Ⓑ SZ 409 852
- Ⓒ SZ 412 861
- Ⓓ SZ 422 868
- Ⓔ SZ 423 858
- Ⓕ SZ 432 844

PUBLIC TRANSPORT Bus services to Brighstone and Calbourne (0871 200 2233)

REFRESHMENTS The Sun: real ale, baguettes, jacket potatoes, hot meals, garden

PUBLIC TOILETS None

ORDNANCE SURVEY MAPS Explorer OL29 (Isle of Wight)

🥾 Walk up the prominent white track from the car park gates onto Mottistone Down. There are wide views to the Long Stone *(see Walk 10)* and the coast to your left, and you may see kestrels or buzzards soaring on the downland wind. Continue for just over ½ mile, to a wicket gate in the wire fence on your right Ⓐ.

Turn right through the gate and follow the bridleway down through the forest to a complex six-way junction. Think of it as a mini-roundabout, take the second exit left, and continue for 200 yds to the next junction. Four broad tracks meet here; a few paces farther on, take the smaller, unsignposted bridleway that bears off to the right into the trees. The path leads gently down the hill, then crosses a wider track and swings to the right along the woodland edge.

Now the bridleway swings back to the left and leads you out of the woods Ⓑ. Carry straight on along the edge of a field and continue onto a wide green lane with views towards Newtown River and the Solent. Soon the lane merges with a gravel road that swings in from your left, and continues to a fork in the track Ⓒ.

Turn right, and follow the gravel road between the buildings at Westover Farm. The road bears left into Withybed Copse, then climbs gently and bears back to the right. Just here, look out for a way-marked stile in the trees on your left; nip across, and follow the path as it winds across wooden boardwalks to a stile on the far edge of the woods. Cross this one, too, and continue across the open field towards the left-hand corner of the woods on the skyline.

Two more waymarked stiles carry you across a farm track and the path continues between wire fences. Another six stiles lead you through the fields to a plank bridge over a brook. Bear right here across the corner of a small field to a stile between two metal gates; nip over, and follow the right-hand field edge to a final gate and stile that leads you out onto the B3401 at Calbourne **D**.

Cross over, turn right, and follow the narrow left-hand verge to the crossroads for a well-earned break at The Sun. Turn right here down Lynch Lane, signposted towards Winkle Street, and *keep an eye open for cars as there's no pavement along this road*. Pass All Saints' Church, set back on the green on your left, then bear left past Winkle Street and the gates of Westover Park. Continue for 650 yds to a small Southern Water building on your left; then, 100 yds later, look out for the signposted bridleway CB20 on your left **E**.

> ✳ The pretty row of cottages overlooking the Caul Bourne is an established Island attraction. Originally called Barrington Row, the cottages have been known as **Winkle Street** for at least 50 years – though it's not certain how the name originated. You can see the **village sheepwash**, last used in the mid-1970s, about halfway down the stream opposite the cottages. The small brass plate fixed to the stonework tells you more about its history.

Turn left up the tree-shaded track towards Brighstone Forest and the Tennyson Trail. After just 200 yds, follow the bridleway as it swings off to the right through a waymarked metal gate and begins the long climb onto Brighstone Down. You've every excuse to stop for a breather, for behind you there's an unfolding panorama that stretches right across Newtown harbour and the Solent to the New Forest.

At the top right-hand corner of the long field, the bridleway dives through a small wooden gate into the shade of Brighstone Forest – but the climb is not over yet. Just keep straight on through the long avenue of beech trees and zigzag right, then left, at the first forest crossroads. The trees are younger here, and the forest clearings bright with willow herb.

The English Channel rises into view as you reach the summit; look away left here to the

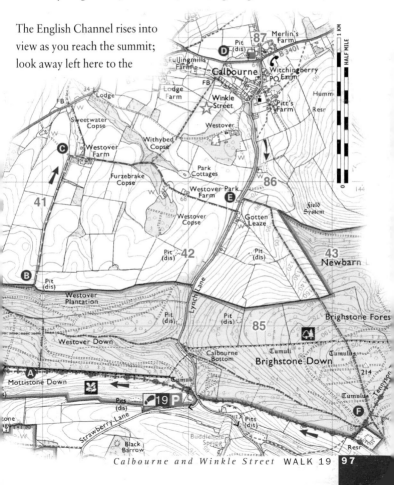

Jubilee Trail, Mottistone Down

Ordnance Survey triangulation pillar which marks the end of your 500-ft climb from the road. Keep straight on past the turning to the pillar, across the scrubby heathland of gorse, heather, holly and stunted beech trees. Now, simply follow the track as it drops off the summit and continues to a junction marked by a four-way signpost **F**.

Turn right here onto the Tennyson Trail, and continue across the next junction towards the Brighstone/Calbourne Road. Follow the gravel road as it bears right and leaves the forest at a wooden gate, then turn to the right as the Tennyson Trail joins the Old Highway towards Mottistone Down. This is the homeward straight, and there are great views for most of the way as the track drops gently down to Lynch Lane. At the road, zigzag briefly left and right to return to the starting point of the walk. ■

> ✳ The **concrete column** on Brighstone Down is one of around 6,500 Ordnance Survey 'triangulation pillars' that once formed the basic framework for all Ordnance Survey mapping. Now, the advent of satellite-based global positioning systems has transformed map-making technology and consigned most of these hilltop pillars to the history books. The 'bench mark' on the side of the pillar is used to fix its height above sea level.

> ❓ *What is the bench mark number on the Ordnance Survey triangulation pillar on Brighstone Down?*

Steaming into Havenstreet

- ■ Varied walking
- ■ picnic areas
- ■ heritage steam railway
- ■ extensive woodlands

Set off through mixed Forestry Commission woodlands and the walk continues through Havenstreet village past the steam railway centre. Now the route threads its way along a wooded bridleway and across open fields to Rowlands Lane. The homeward trek follows this quiet country lane north, before branching off across farmland and back through Havenstreet for a woodland finale.

walk 20

Havenstreet Railway Station

walk 20

START Firestone Copse car park

DISTANCE 5$\frac{1}{2}$ miles (8.8km)

TIME 3 hours

PARKING Forestry Commission car park at the start

ROUTE FEATURES This walk includes a dozen stiles and a mile of walking on country lanes, making it less suitable for groups or families with children. Please lead dogs along the roads, as well as through the farms

GPS WAYPOINTS

SZ 558 910
Ⓐ SZ 560 903
Ⓑ SZ 558 901
Ⓒ SZ 554 896
Ⓓ SZ 542 878
Ⓔ SZ 551 878
Ⓕ SZ 563 881
Ⓖ SZ 565 896

PUBLIC TRANSPORT Isle of Wight steam railway trains (01983 882204) connect Havenstreet with the Island Line at Smallbrook Junction. Limited bus service from Newport and Ryde (0871 200 2233)

REFRESHMENTS The White Hart: Real ales, meals, family garden; Havenstreet Station cafeteria: teas, coffees, lunches, ice creams

PUBLIC TOILETS For pub and railway patrons only

ORDNANCE SURVEY MAPS Explorer OL29 (Isle of Wight)

Leave the car park between the picnic tables and set off down the gravelled path to the woods. Continue for 250 yds, then turn right and follow the path along the woodland edge for another 100 yds as far as the stile on your left. Nip across, then zigzag left and right over a second stile onto the narrow, signposted path as it pulls clear of the woods along the edge of a couple of fields. At length the path bears left and briefly follows a gravelled driveway before reaching the village road opposite Holmdale House old folk's home Ⓐ.

Turn right, pass the White Hart and the impressive Northbrooke House nursing home Ⓑ, and follow the village road under the railway bridge to Havenstreet Station. *Take care along this section, as there's only a short length of pavement.*

The Isle of Wight steam railway has all the ingredients for a great family day out. At Havenstreet you'll find beautifully restored station buildings straight out of the 1920s, as well as a museum, souvenir shop, and licensed refreshment room. There's a recreation field, too, where you're welcome to picnic or enjoy your own ball games.

But, of course, the main attraction is the vintage steam trains that puff through Havenstreet on most days between April and September. Your ticket buys unlimited travel for the day, and there are special fares for families.

About 75 yds beyond the station entrance, fork left onto bridleway N18 **C** towards Combley and Arreton Down. A quiet, leafy stretch ushers in just over a mile of easy walking as you follow the bridleway all the way to Combley Farm. Follow the track as it bears left, then right, through the farmyard and continue for another 150 yds.

Double back through the waymarked wicket gate on your left **Ⓓ**, and head diagonally up the slope towards the far corner of the field. Bear left here through the waymarked field gate, follow the track along the left-hand edge of this large open field, and continue into the next field through a gap in the hedge. Almost at the far side of this second field, the track swings left through a metal gate; leave it here, and follow the bridleway as it bears right towards a similar gate 100 yds ahead of you. From here, follow the waymarked route across the middle of the next field to the metal gates on the far side. There's a farm crossroads here **Ⓔ**, and your way lies along the bridleway straight ahead.

Continue along the waymarked track as it zigzags left and right past Duxmore Farm. Although the bridleway downgrades to a footpath here, it follows a wide farm lane with grass along the centre. Continue past a field gate and stile, and follow a line of wooden electricity poles across the middle of an open field. A small wooden gate on the far side of the field leads you to a waymarked T- junction. Turn left, nip over the stile beside Little Duxmore, then turn right and follow the wider farm track leading out onto Rowlands Lane **Ⓕ**.

Turn left onto the road, pass the attractive Rowlands Farm on your right, and continue for ¾ mile to the railway bridge. *There's no pavement here so, although traffic is usually light, do take care and watch out for the occasional car.*

Havenstreet, White Hart Inn

Just beyond the bridge, turn left over the stile at Bridge Farm onto footpath R9 **G**. Two more stiles follow in quick succession; now, follow the footpath towards the far left-hand corner of the field, where you'll find a stile set deep in the hedge at the entrance to a small wood. Jump the stile, and follow the narrow woodland path to a footbridge and stile. Cross over, then bear left through the next field to a double stile at the top left-hand corner. Nip across, turn left along the short side of a long thin field to another pair of stiles, and continue beside the hedge on your left to yet another stile straight ahead. Go over this one, too, continuing up the gravelled drive past Ivy Dene to Havenstreet village **B**.

Turn right, and follow the road past the White Hart as far as the telephone box on your left. Turn left here, and retrace your outward steps back to the start. ∎

★ Havenstreet Station has been the home of the Isle of Wight **steam railway** for more than 30 years. Five years after British Railways closed the line in 1966, the company began restoring the track, buildings and trains. A new terminus was opened at Wootton in 1986, and by 1991 the rails once again stretched eastwards through Ashey to Smallbrook Junction. With its **Victorian locomotives and carriages**, the line is now one of Britain's premier heritage railways.

? *What is the height restriction under Havenstreet railway bridge?*

Further Information

Walking Safety

Always take with you both warm and waterproof clothing and sufficient food and drink. Wear suitable footwear such as strong walking boots or shoes that give a good grip over stony ground, on slippery slopes and in muddy conditions. Try to obtain a local weather forecast and bear it in mind before you start. Do not be afraid to abandon your proposed route and return to your starting point in the event of a sudden and unexpected deterioration in the weather.

Chilton Chine cliffs

All the walks described in this book will be safe to do, given due care and respect, even during the winter. Indeed, a crisp, fine winter day often provides perfect walking conditions, with firm ground underfoot and a clarity of light unique to that time of the year.

The most difficult hazard likely to be encountered is mud, especially when walking along woodland and field paths, farm tracks and bridleways – the latter in particular can often get churned up by cyclists and horses. In summer, an additional difficulty may be narrow and overgrown paths, particularly along the edges of cultivated fields. Neither should constitute a major problem provided that the appropriate footwear is worn.

Global Positioning System (GPS)
What is GPS?
Global Positioning System, or GPS for short, is a fully-functional navigation system that uses a network of satellites to calculate positions, which are then transmitted to hand-held receivers. By measuring the time it takes a signal to reach the receiver, the distance from the satellite can be estimated. Repeat this with several satellites and the receiver can then triangulate its position, in effect telling the receiver exactly where you are, in any weather, day or night, anywhere on Earth.

GPS information, in the form of grid reference data, is increasingly being used in Pathfinder® guidebooks, and many readers find the positional accuracy GPS affords a reassurance, although its greatest benefit comes when you are walking in remote, open countryside or through forests.

GPS has become a vital global utility, indispensable for modern navigation on land, sea and air around the world, as well as an important tool for map-making and land surveying.

Useful Organisations

Blackgang Chine
Blackgang Chine, near Ventnor,
Isle of Wight PO38 2HN
Tel: 01983 730052
www.blackgangchine.com

Brading Roman Villa
Morton Old Road, Brading,
Isle of Wight PO36 0EN
Tel: 01983 406223
www.bradingromanvilla.org.uk

Campaign to Protect Rural England
128 Southwark Street,
London SE1 0SW
Tel: 020 7981 2800
www.cpre.org.uk

English Heritage
Customer Services Department,
PO Box 569, Swindon
SN2 2YP
Tel: 0870 333 1181
www.english-heritage.org.uk

Forestry Commission
South East England Forest District,
Bucks Horn Oak, Farnham, Surrey
GU10 4LS
Tel: 01420 23666
www.forestry.gov.uk

Fort Victoria Country Park
Fort Victoria, Yarmouth,
Isle of Wight
Tel: 01983 823893
www.fortvictoria.co.uk

Isle of Wight Council
Public Rights of Way, Coastal
Centre, Dudley Road, Ventnor,
PO38 1EJ
Tel: 01983 821000
www.iwight.com

Isle of Wight Donkey Sanctuary
Lower Winstone Farm, Wroxall,
Isle of Wight PO38 3AA
Tel: 01983 852693
www.iwdonkey-sanctuary.com

Blackgang Chine

Isle of Wight Steam Railway
The Railway Station,
Havenstreet,
Isle of Wight
PO33 4DS
Tel: 01983 882204
www.iwsteamrailway.co.uk

Isle of Wight Tourism
Isle of Wight Council,
County Hall, High Street,
Newport
PO30 1UD
Tel: 01983 813813
www.islandbreaks.co.uk

Hampshire & Isle of Wight Wildlife Trust
Beechcroft House, Vicarage Lane,
Curdridge, Hampshire SO32 2DP
Tel: 01489 774400
www.hwt.org.uk

National Rail Enquiries
Tel: 08457 48 49 50
www.nationalrail.co.uk

The National Trust
PO Box 39, Warrington WA5 7WD
Tel: 0870 458 4000
www.nationaltrust.org.uk

Natural England
Northminster House,
Peterborough PE1 1UA
Tel: 0845 600 3078
www.naturalengland.org.uk

Nunwell House
Coach Lane, Brading, Isle of Wight
Tel: 01983 407240

Needles Park
Alum Bay, Isle of Wight PO39 0JD
Tel: 0870 458 0022
www.theneedles.co.uk

Ordnance Survey
Romsey Road,
Southampton
SO16 4GU
Tel: 08456 05 05 05
www.ordnancesurvey.co.uk

Red Funnel Ferries
12 Bugle Street,
Southampton
SO14 2JY
Tel: 0844 844 9988
www.redfunnel.co.uk

Isle of Wight Donkey Sanctuary

**Royal Society for the
Protection of Birds**
The Lodge, Sandy,
Bedfordshire
SG19 2DL
Tel: 01767 680551
www.rspb.org.uk

St Catherine's Lighthouse
Niton, Ventnor,
Isle of Wight
Tel: 01983 855069
www.trinityhouse.co.uk

Southern Vectis
Nelson Road, Newport PO30 1RD
Tel: 01983 827000
www.islandbuses.info

WightLink Ferries
PO Box 59, Portsmouth PO1 2XB
Tel: 0871 376 1000
www.wightlink.co.uk

The Woodland Trust
Autumn Park, Dysart Road,
Grantham, Lincs NG31 6LL
Tel: 01476 581135
www.woodland-trust.org.uk

Ordnance Survey Maps
Explorer OL29 (Isle of Wight)

Answers to Questions

Walk 1: The wireless pioneer, Guglielmo Marconi.

Walk 2: One shilling (5p) a year.

Walk 3: The church is dedicated to St John the Evangelist.

Walk 4: All these species are found at the Norton Spit Site of Special
Scientific Interest.

Walk 5: 1928.

Walk 6: More than 2000.

Walk 7: The Tennyson Memorial was erected on the site of the old
beacon in 1897.

Walk 8: £200.

Walk 9: The gate was built in memory of William Sells, Rector of Niton
between 1890 and 1918.

Walk 10: The churchyard is mown annually at the end of July, after the wild flowers and grasses have seeded.

Walk 11: October 6, 1892.

Walk 12: The name is probably Saxon, and is believed to mean 'Alfred's Farm'.

Walk 13: Rev Stobart was the vicar of Carisbrooke, 1902-1914.

Walk 14: August 1998.

Walk 15: Mrs E Smith, of Mill Farm, Bembridge, in 1958.

Walk 16: Ryde.

Walk 17: No parking is allowed within 250 ft (76m).

Walk 18: The last collection is at 12 noon, Monday to Friday.

Walk 19: OSBM S2492.

Walk 20: 13ft 6in (4.1m).

Godshill, Bat's Wing tearoom

Crimson Walking Guides

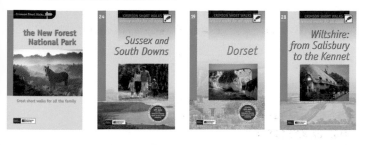